ECONOMICS AND THE ENVIRONMENT

EARTH • AT • RISK

EARTH • AT • RISK

ECONOMICS AND THE ENVIRONMENT

by Jake Goldberg

Introduction by
Russell E. Train

Chairman of the Board of
Directors,
World Wildlife Fund and
The Conservation Foundation

CHELSEA HOUSE PUBLISHERS
new york philadelphia

CHELSEA HOUSE PUBLISHERS
EDITOR-IN-CHIEF: Richard S. Papale
MANAGING EDITOR: Karyn Gullen Browne
COPY CHIEF: Philip Koslow
PICTURE EDITOR: Adrian G. Allen
ART DIRECTOR: Nora Wertz
MANUFACTURING DIRECTOR: Gerald Levine
SYSTEMS MANAGER: Lindsey Ottman
PRODUCTION COORDINATOR: Marie Claire Cebrián-Ume

EARTH AT RISK
SENIOR EDITOR: Jake Goldberg

Staff for *Economics and the Environment*
COPY EDITOR: Margaret Dornfeld
EDITORIAL ASSISTANT: Robert Kimball Green
PICTURE RESEARCHER: Villette Harris
SENIOR DESIGNER: Marjorie Zaum
COVER ILLUSTRATION: Bill Donahey

3   5   7   9   8   6   4

Library of Congress Cataloging-in-Publication Data
Goldberg, Jake.
  Economics and the Environment/by Jake Goldberg; introduction
  by Russell E. Train.
    p. cm.—(Earth at risk)
  Includes bibliographical references and index.
  Summary: Examines the role of economics in preserving or
destroying the environment and conflicts between companies and
environmentalists.
  ISBN   0-7910-1594-7
          0-7910-1619-6(pbk.)
    1. Environmental policy—Economic aspects—Juvenile
literature. [1. Environmental policy—Economic aspects. 2.
Environmental protection—Economic aspects.]
  I. Title. II. Series.   92-10593
  HC79.E5G627 1992   CIP
  333.7'2—dc20   AC

C O N T E N T S

INTRODUCTION

Russell E. Train

Administrator, Environmental Protection Agency, 1973 to
1977; Chairman of the Board of Directors, World Wildlife
Fund and the Conservation Foundation

There is a growing realization that human activities increasingly
are threatening the health of the natural systems that make life possible
on this planet. Humankind has the power to alter nature fundamentally,
perhaps irreversibly.

This stark reality was dramatized in January 1989 when *Time*
magazine named Earth the "Planet of the Year." In the same year, the
Exxon *Valdez* disaster sparked public concern over the effects of human
activity on vulnerable ecosystems when a thick blanket of crude oil
coated the shores and wildlife of Prince William Sound in Alaska. And,
no doubt, the 20th anniversary celebration of Earth Day in April 1990
renewed broad public interest in environmental issues still further. It is
no accident then that many people are calling the years between 1990
and 2000 the "Decade of the Environment."

And this is not merely a case of media hype, for the 1990s will
truly be a time when the people of the planet Earth learn the meaning of
the phrase "everything is connected to everything else" in the natural
and man-made systems that sustain our lives. This will be a period when
more people will understand that burning a tree in Amazonia adversely
affects the global atmosphere just as much as the exhaust from the cars
that fill our streets and expressways.

Central to our understanding of environmental issues is the
need to recognize the complexity of the problems we face and the

relationships between environmental and other needs in our society. Global warming provides an instructive example. Controlling emissions of carbon dioxide, the principal greenhouse gas, will involve efforts to reduce the use of fossil fuels to generate electricity. Such a reduction will include energy conservation and the promotion of alternative energy sources, such as nuclear and solar power.

The automobile contributes significantly to the problem. We have the choice of switching to more energy-efficient autos and, in the longer run, of choosing alternative automotive power systems and relying more on mass transit. This will require different patterns of land use and development, patterns that are less transportation and energy intensive.

In agriculture, rice paddies and cattle are major sources of greenhouse gases. Recent experiments suggest that universally used nitrogen fertilizers may inhibit the ability of natural soil organisms to take up methane, thus contributing tremendously to the atmospheric loading of that gas—one of the major culprits in the global warming scenario.

As one explores the various parameters of today's pressing environmental challenges, it is possible to identify some areas where we have made some progress. We have taken important steps to control gross pollution over the past two decades. What I find particularly encouraging is the growing environmental consciousness and activism by today's youth. In many communities across the country, young people are working together to take their environmental awareness out of the classroom and apply it to everyday problems. Successful recycling and tree-planting projects have been launched as a result of these budding environmentalists who have committed themselves to a cleaner environment. Citizen action, activated by youthful enthusiasm, was largely responsible for the fast-food industry's switch from rainforest to domestic beef, for pledges from important companies in the tuna industry to use fishing techniques that would not harm dolphins, and for the recent announcement by the McDonald's Corporation to phase out polystyrene "clam shell" hamburger containers.

Despite these successes, much remains to be done if we are to make ours a truly healthy environment. Even a short list of persistent issues includes problems such as acid rain, ground-level ozone and smog, and airborne toxins; groundwater protection and nonpoint sources of pollution, such as runoff from farms and city streets; wetlands protection; hazardous waste dumps; and solid waste disposal, waste minimization, and recycling.

Similarly, there is an unfinished agenda in the natural resources area: effective implementation of newly adopted management plans for national forests; strengthening the wildlife refuge system; national park management, including addressing the growing pressure of development on lands surrounding the parks; implementation of the Endangered Species Act; wildlife trade problems, such as that involving elephant ivory; and ensuring adequate sustained funding for these efforts at all levels of government. All of these issues are before us today; most will continue in one form or another through the year 2000.

Each of these challenges to environmental quality and our health requires a response that recognizes the complex nature of the problem. Narrowly conceived solutions will not achieve lasting results. Often it seems that when we grab hold of one part of the environmental balloon, an unsightly and threatening bulge appears somewhere else.

The higher environmental issues arise on the national agenda, the more important it is that we are armed with the best possible knowledge of the economic costs of undertaking particular environmental programs and the costs associated with not undertaking them. Our society is not blessed with unlimited resources, and tough choices are going to have to be made. These should be informed choices.

All too often, environmental objectives are seen as at cross-purposes with other considerations vital to our society. Thus, environmental protection is often viewed as being in conflict with economic growth, with energy needs, with agricultural productions, and so on. The time has come when environmental considerations must be fully integrated into every nation's priorities.

One area that merits full legislative attention is energy efficiency. The United States is one of the least energy efficient of all the industrialized nations. Japan, for example, uses far less energy per unit of gross national product than the United States does. Of course, a country as large as the United States requires large amounts of energy for transportation. However, there is still a substantial amount of excess energy used, and this excess constitutes waste. More fuel-efficient autos and home heating systems would save millions of barrels of oil, or their equivalent, each year. And air pollutants, including greenhouse gases, could be significantly reduced by increased efficiency in industry.

I suspect that the environmental problem that comes closest to home for most of us is the problem of what to do with trash. All over the world, communities are wrestling with the problem of waste disposal. Landfill sites are rapidly filling to capacity. No one wants a trash and garbage dump near home. As William Ruckelshaus, former EPA administrator and now in the waste management business, puts it, "Everyone wants you to pick up the garbage and no one wants you to put it down!"

At the present time, solid waste programs emphasize the regulation of disposal, setting standards for landfills, and so forth. In the decade ahead, we must shift our emphasis from regulating waste disposal to an overall reduction in its volume. We must look at the entire waste stream, including product design and packaging. We must avoid creating waste in the first place. To the greatest extent possible, we should then recycle any waste that is produced. I believe that, while most of us enjoy our comfortable way of life and have no desire to change things, we also know in our hearts that our "disposable society" has allowed us to become pretty soft.

Land use is another domestic issue that might well attract legislative attention by the year 2000. All across the United States, communities are grappling with the problem of growth. All too often, growth imposes high costs on the environment—the pollution of aquifers; the destruction of wetlands; the crowding of shorelines; the loss of wildlife habitat; and the loss of those special places, such as a historic structure or area, that give a community a sense of identity. It is worth noting that growth is not only the product of economic development but of population movement. By the year 2010, for example, experts predict that 75% of all Americans will live within 50 miles of a coast.

It is important to keep in mind that we are all made vulnerable by environmental problems that cross international borders. Of course, the most critical global conservation problems are the destruction of tropical forests and the consequent loss of their biological capital. Some scientists have calculated extinction rates as high as 11 species per hour. All agree that the loss of species has never been greater than at the present time; not even the disappearance of the dinosaurs can compare to today's rate of extinction.

In addition to species extinctions, the loss of tropical forests may represent as much as 20% of the total carbon dioxide loadings to the atmosphere. Clearly, any international approach to the problem of global warming must include major efforts to stop the destruction of forests and to manage those that remain on a renewable basis. Debt for nature swaps, which the World Wildlife Fund has pioneered in Costa Rica, Ecuador, Madagascar, and the Philippines, provide a useful mechanism for promoting such conservation objectives.

Global environmental issues inevitably will become the principal focus in international relations. But the single overriding issue facing the world community today is how to achieve a sustainable balance between growing human populations and the earth's natural systems. If you travel as frequently as I do in the developing countries of Latin America, Africa, and Asia, it is hard to escape the reality that expanding human populations are seriously weakening the earth's resource base. Rampant deforestation, eroding soils, spreading deserts, loss of biological diversity, the destruction of fisheries, and polluted and degraded urban environments threaten to spread environmental impoverishment, particularly in the tropics, where human population growth is greatest.

It is important to recognize that environmental degradation and human poverty are closely linked. Impoverished people desperate for land on which to grow crops or graze cattle are destroying forests and overgrazing even more marginal land. These people become trapped in a vicious downward spiral. They have little choice but to continue to overexploit the weakened resources available to them. Continued abuse of these lands only diminishes their productivity. Throughout the developing world, alarming amounts of land rendered useless by over-grazing and poor agricultural practices have become virtual wastelands, yet human numbers continue to multiply in these areas.

From Bangladesh to Haiti, we are confronted with an increasing number of ecological basket cases. In the Philippines, a traditional focus of U.S. interest, environmental devastation is widespread as defores-tation, soil erosion, and the destruction of coral reefs and fisheries combine with the highest population growth rate in Southeast Asia.

Controlling human population growth is the key factor in the environmental equation. World population is expected to at least double to about 11 billion before leveling off. Most of this growth will occur in the poorest nations of the developing world. I would hope that the United States will once again become a strong advocate of international efforts to promote family planning. Bringing human populations into a sustainable balance with their natural resource base must be a vital objective of U.S. foreign policy.

Foreign economic assistance, the program of the Agency for International Development (AID), can become a potentially powerful tool for arresting environmental deterioration in developing countries. People who profess to care about global environmental problems— the loss of biological diversity, the destruction of tropical forests, the greenhouse effect, the impoverishment of the marine environment, and so on—should be strong supporters of foreign aid planning and the principles of sustainable development urged by the World Commission on Environment and Development, the "Brundtland Commission."

If sustainability is to be the underlying element of overseas assistance programs, so too must it be a guiding principle in people's practices at home. Too often we think of sustainable development only in terms of the resources of other countries. We have much that we can and should be doing to promote long-term sustainability in our own resource management. The conflict over our own rainforests, the old growth forests of the Pacific Northwest, illustrates this point.

The decade ahead will be a time of great activity on the environmental front, both globally and domestically. I sincerely believe we will be tested as we have been only in times of war and during the Great Depression. We must set goals for the year 2000 that will challenge both the American people and the world community.

Despite the complexities ahead, I remain an optimist. I am confident that if we collectively commit ourselves to a clean, healthy environment we can surpass the achievements of the 1980s and meet the serious challenges that face us in the coming decades. I hope that today's students will recognize their significant role in and responsibility for bringing about change and will rise to the occasion to improve the quality of our global environment.

Chico Mendez (1944–1988)

ECOLOGY AND ECONOMICS

On December 22, 1988, at the start of the rainy season, in the village of Xapuri in the Brazilian state of Acre, in the heart of the rainforest, Chico Mendez, leader of the National Rubber Tappers Council, left his wife Ilza, his children, and his bodyguards behind, stepped through the door of his house, and was shot dead by *pistoleiros*—gunmen hired by Darli Alves and his son Darci, wealthy local ranchers.

Mendez had been a marked man for some time, and he understood the risks he was taking. His union of rubber tappers, or *seringueiros*, was fighting to save the rainforest. Allied with local Indians and Brazil nut pickers, the union wanted to do away with individual land grants to forest workers. Often, wealthy ranchers would intimidate the workers into selling them the grants, and the rubber tappers lost their land and their source of livelihood. Instead, the union wanted to establish extractive reserves—protected areas of the forest that could be harvested but not broken up and sold piecemeal. In February 1988, the rubber tappers had won an important victory with the establishment of the first such extractive reserve at São Luis de Remanso.

The union's program constituted a great threat to the Alves family and other ranchers in the area, who wanted to burn and clear the rainforest to create grazing land for cattle. It was of no concern to them that the burning of the forest threatened the world's climate, or that with the disappearance of the forest many as yet unknown species of life were being wiped out, or that small forest growers produced 80% of Brazil's food supply. Nor did it seem to matter to them that raising beef for export was not even very profitable, for it was possible to get rich from cattle ranching simply by taking advantage of government subsidies and tax incentives. For the Alves family—wealthy and powerful, protected by corrupt politicians and policemen in a remote area where the law was ineffective at best—the simplest solution was to murder their opponents.

In March 1989, after an extraordinary international outcry, the Brazilian government was forced to indict Darli and Darci Alves for the murder of Chico Mendez. At the trial, Darci Alves broke down and confessed to the crime, and the two men were convicted. But it was a sad, inconclusive, and rare triumph for the people of the rainforest. In their 1990 book *The Fate of the Forest*, Susanna Hecht and Alexander Cockburn point out that though "more than 1,000 rural organizers and workers have died in conflicts" since the emergence of Brazil's civilian government in 1985, "less than ten" of these cases have gone to trial. And the rainforest continues to be ravaged.

The events surrounding the death of Chico Mendez dramatically illustrate the relationship between economic activity and environmental degradation. The Brazilian government's support of cattle ranching and the production of beef for export is in part the result of its huge international debt. By increasing its exports, the government hopes to acquire large amounts of foreign currency to pay back this debt. The rubber tappers and nut pickers, on the other hand, most of whom are poor emigrants from other parts of Brazil where there is no land to farm and few jobs to work at, desperately need the rainforest to sustain them.

Around the globe, humankind's economic activities and the competition for wealth among nations contribute daily to the destruction of the environment and the depletion of natural resources. As environmental problems escalate, environmentalists and economists are beginning to understand that they are looking at the same problem from different points of view.

For example, environmentalists are concerned about the destruction of the rainforests and the climate change brought about by this destruction, whereas economists study the patterns of debt and poverty in tropical countries that drive people to burn the forests and clear the land. Environmentalists demand the removal of chemical pollutants and toxic wastes from the air and water, but economists worry about the effect of such a clean-up on an industry's costs and the price of its products.

Deforestation, the *erosion* of soil, urban blight, disease, *acid rain*, *global warming*, the extinction of species—all these environmental issues are viewed by economists as facets of a greater crisis that results from global problems in agricultural and industrial production. Economists search for the causes of environmental destruction by studying imbalances in world trade, international debt, inequities in the worldwide division of energy resources and technology, and the unequal distribution of wealth, power, and land between and within nations.

As environmental destruction is caused by the productive activity of human beings, it is only through an understanding of

that productive activity that humankind can hope to contain
and reverse the destruction. Otherwise, sooner or later, the result
will be the exhaustion of *natural resources* and the collapse of
economic systems. The United Nations–sponsored World Commission on Environment and Development, in its 1987 report
entitled *Our Common Future*, stated:

> It is impossible to separate economic
> development issues from environment issues; many
> forms of development erode the environmental resources
> upon which they must be based, and environmental
> degradation can undermine economic development.
> Poverty is a major cause and effect of global environ-
> mental problems. It is therefore futile to attempt to deal
> with environmental problems without a broader
> perspective that encompasses the factors underlying
> world poverty and international inequality.

This book will examine the crisis of the environment from
this broader economic perspective. It will attempt to reorient
readers with the true nature of this crisis. The destruction of the
natural world is both the result of human misery arising from
social and economic inequities and the cause of further suffering.
These problems are not caused simply by stupidity, indifference,
lack of foresight, or selfishness, though these are all factors. Underlying most environmental problems is the desperate, driving
force of economic need. Achieving a safe, clean, and livable
environment means much more than just having breathable air
and drinkable water, or saving the elephants and the whales, or
even protecting the ozone layer and the rainforests. It means

achieving a stable economic and political order in which all the world's peoples have adequate food, shelter, health care, energy, education, security, political freedom, and outlets for cultural and spiritual expression.

In order to be both economically and ecologically efficient, this new world economic order will also have to be *sustainable*. It must use only those natural resources that are renewable and must return to nature only the kinds and amounts of waste that a healthy environment can absorb. In the past, people viewed the need to use resources efficiently mainly as a problem for individual businesses and households trying to reduce their costs. Now, however, more and more people are coming to view efficiency as an essential concept for the survival of the global community. As a result, economists are trying to learn how natural systems work or fail to work, and how that affects economic activity. Environmentalists are trying to master the workings of economic systems in order to understand and prevent environmental degradation. The disciplines of economics and ecology are coming closer together.

Rows of durable consumer goods such as washing machines, refrigerators, and television sets prove just how productive modern industrial society is. But can this affluence be sustained in the face of dwindling natural resources, rising energy prices, and environmental pollution?

chapter 1

THE MEASURE OF
OUR SUCCESS

For the last five decades, most nations have been in agreement about the importance of certain basic numbers as measures of the performance of their economies. By far the most important such number is the *gross national product*, or GNP, which is defined as the total monetary value of all the finished goods and services produced by a country in one year. Government economists constantly receive information from factories, farms, and businesses, and every year they calculate the total value of all the automobiles produced, all the airplanes, all the television sets, the cameras, the books, the furniture, the bicycles, the washing machines, the pots and pans, the matchsticks, candy bars, and electric toothbrushes. They add in the value of all the fruit, vegetables, meat, and milk sent to market, the coats and clothing sold in department stores, and the income earned by service businesses such as restaurants, hairdressers, plumbers, interior decorators, insurance companies, street vendors, grave-diggers, and rainmakers.

GNP includes only finished or final goods—those offered to consumers—in order to avoid the error of *double counting,* which would make the gross national product look much larger than it really is. It would be incorrect to add to GNP the value of the steel produced for the automobile industry, because the value of that steel is included in the price of the finished car. It would be wrong to add in the value of chicken feed, because, again, that value would be included in the price of each supermarket chicken. Nails sold to consumers in hardware stores would be included in GNP; those sold to house builders would not. The value of most oil would not be included; the value of most gasoline would. Only finished products are counted—products whose price is figured as a cost in the manufacture of other products must be subtracted from GNP. Clearly, calculating GNP is an immensely complicated task.

To this vast and varied array of *consumption* goods, economists add several other lump sums that reflect a nation's productive wealth. They add the expenditures of *government*. A certain portion of people's income is taken from them in taxes and spent by national and local governments to pay for goods and services that most consumers could not afford as individuals—missiles, tanks, fighter planes, space shuttles, bridges and highways, law enforcement and postal services, schools and libraries, and trash collection.

Also included in GNP are *exports*. Some of the goods a country produces are sold abroad in other countries, but they still count as part of the producing country's national wealth. Of course, *imports*, goods produced abroad and sold "here," must be subtracted from exports to show the *net value* of exports. If a country imports more than it exports, as has happened in the United States in recent years, net exports will have a negative value, creating an unfavorable *balance of trade*. This could result in a *trade deficit*, in which a country owes more to foreign producers than foreign consumers owe to it. In any case, if net exports are a negative value, they will reduce the size of GNP.

Finally, economists add in *investment*. Investment in economics has a specific meaning beyond simply the money placed in a savings account or the stocks and bonds purchased with the hope of earning high returns. It concerns what is done with these sums of money after they are deposited or invested in banks, savings and loan institutions, and corporations. Businesses borrow and use this money to manufacture a special and very costly category of products known as *capital goods*. Capital goods are not finished goods and are not sold to or enjoyed by consumers. Neither are they intermediate goods such as raw materials or unassembled parts or animal feed. They are *the goods used to make other goods* and include factory buildings, blast furnaces, machine tools, research laboratories, and all the mechanized gadgets that press, cut, shape, form, sew, drill, extrude, or weld the products people need. These goods do not appear in the consumer marketplace, but they are vital to measuring not only a nation's wealth but its ability to increase that wealth in the future. Though it does not *at first* create even one new television set or put even one new automobile into the showroom, investment is a good measure of a nation's future ability to expand its producing capacity.

Of course, if a clothing manufacturer bought ten new sewing machines but failed to subtract the value of three old sewing machines that wore out, his estimate of how much he has invested to expand his business would be erroneously high. Similarly, there is no net economic growth if a businessperson simply rebuilds a factory that has burned down. Capital goods

that lose their usefulness fall under the category of *depreciation,*
and depreciation must be subtracted from total investment to
determine *net investment.*

Furthermore, the value of *all* the products and services
included in GNP must be adjusted for *inflation,* the tendency in
market economies for the price of goods to increase over time.
That is to say, money itself decreases in value, and a given
amount will purchase fewer products. If, for example, in 1990
consumers purchased $45 billion worth of automobiles, but in
1991 they purchased $50 billion worth of automobiles, it does
not necessarily mean that more automobiles were sold, for the
price of each individual automobile may have risen. When the
prices of all these goods are adjusted for inflation, *nominal* GNP
becomes *real* GNP, and economists have finally arrived at a
number that tells them something useful about a nation's productivity. By comparing GNP from one year to the next, economists can determine the *rate of economic growth* as a percentage
increase or decrease over or under the previous year's GNP. By
dividing total GNP by the population, economists can determine
per capita GNP, or the amount of wealth created by or for each
citizen.

In 1988, the gross national product of the United States
was approximately $4,862,000,000,000, or almost $5 trillion, or
$5 thousand billion. The magnitude of such a number is over-
whelming; the wealth produced by an industrialized nation like
the United States in one year is enormous.

During that same year, Japan's GNP was approximately
$2,577,000,000,000, about half that of the United States, and the
GNP of West Germany was about $1,131,000,000,000. Of
course, as these countries have much smaller populations than

the United States, per capita GNP—the average amount of individual wealth created—is much closer to that of the American citizen than total GNP would indicate.

The gross national product is much more than a number. It is a commitment to a particular definition of prosperity and well-being. It has also been used as a political weapon. For nearly two decades, from the late 1950s to the late 1970s, until stagnation in the economy of the Soviet Union rendered the debate meaningless, GNP figures were part of the propaganda war between capitalist and communist nations, with each economy claiming higher rates of economic growth. The debate was fierce, but both groups of nations shared the belief that whichever had the greatest rate of GNP growth had the superior economic system and therefore could provide its people with the best standard of living. It was taken for granted that economic growth is a good thing and that "progress" could be measured in terms of increasing output and the production of larger and larger amounts of material goods.

WHAT GNP DOES NOT MEASURE

But is a nation or a society nothing more than the *things* it produces? Can quality of life be measured exclusively in terms of who makes the most of everything—from liquor and pet food and cosmetics to fur coats and jewelry and nuclear warheads? Increasingly, economists influenced by environmental concerns are pointing out shortcomings in what the gross national product measures. The value of products that actually degrade the quality of life are often added to GNP as a positive gain in national wealth. The value of cigarettes and tobacco products figures into

GNP as a plus, though cigarette smoking is a major cause of cancer. Ironically, GNP also includes as a gain in wealth the price of health care systems and health insurance plans, though a portion of these services goes toward undoing the "benefits" of cigarettes. GNP also puts a premium on pure quantity and poor quality. "Shoddy appliances that need frequent repair and fast replacement, for instance," write Lester Brown, Christopher Flavin, and Sandra Postel of the Worldwatch Institute, a research group that studies issues involving the environment and the economy, "raise the GNP more than a well-crafted product that lasts, even though the latter is really more valuable."

Because it is a measure of prices, GNP does not include the value of unpaid labor, such as that of homemakers in cooking, housekeeping, and child-rearing activities; or the work people do for each other without any cash changing hands. Nor can GNP measure the value of illegal and unreported activities such as drug dealing and prostitution. Some of these deficiencies have long been recognized and accepted by economists as unavoidable. But from an ecological perspective, there are two very important failings of GNP that are becoming harder to ignore.

The first failing concerns what economists call *external costs.* In a situation where there are many competing producers of a certain product, competition will drive down the price of that product, and producers must minimize their costs to earn profits. This is a feature of the *law of supply and demand,* a basic economic law that describes how producers and consumers behave in the marketplace. No businessperson will want to pay any costs that he or she can avoid paying. The goal is to keep such costs *external* to the company's accounting system. External costs are not reflected in GNP.

External costs abound in market economies, and many of them are costs to the environment. For example, the price of a refrigerator does not include any portion of the cost of treating new cases of skin cancer, though when the refrigerator is disposed of at the end of its useful life, the chlorofluorocarbon gases in its cooling unit may leak into the atmosphere and attack the stratospheric ozone layer, which shields living things from harmful ultraviolet radiation. A farmer must pay for the fertilizers and pesticides that make high crop yields possible, but neither that farmer nor the manufacturer of those chemicals bears any of the cost of cleaning toxins from the surrounding soils and streams when the chemicals are dispersed by rain. The prices utility companies charge for electricity do not include the cost of damage to lakes and forests from the acid rain their power plants create. Paper manufacturers use chlorine-based bleaching compounds to turn brown wood chips into white paper, then discharge dioxin-laden waste water into nearby rivers, where communities downstream bear the cost of degraded water supplies. When, after several accidents, designers of nuclear power plants were

This coal-fired power plant in Montana helps to generate the large amounts of cheap electricity needed by American industry, but who pays the "external" costs of air pollution?

forced to consider the costs of emergency containment and decontamination, evacuation schemes, and safe radioactive waste disposal, nuclear power no longer seemed so economically attractive an energy source.

Economists call the type of calculations described above the *true costs* of production, and though it is not easy to measure these costs, more and more people are trying. Ecologists like to point out that pollution and waste are the unavoidable end products of economic activity. Although a rapidly growing, high-GNP economy in all likelihood will engage in the wholesale poisoning of its environment, thereby degrading the lives of its citizens, the conventional gauge of its prosperity—the GNP—will show no sign of danger.

Since the environmental movement first became a powerful political force in the early 1970s, national and local governments have been called upon to impose external costs on unwilling producers by force of law, backed up by fines and penalties. The Clean Air Acts of 1970 and 1977 set emission limits for sulfur and nitrogen oxides, carbon monoxide, unburned hydrocarbons, ozone, and lead. These laws have definitely helped to clean up the air, but they have forced power plants to install expensive sulfur "scrubbing" equipment in their exhaust systems or to buy more expensive low-sulfur coal. Automobile manufacturers in the United States are required to fit exhaust systems with catalytic converters to reduce lead emissions. Federal rules that mandate minimum gas mileages make the engines of these cars more expensive to design and build.

Other government strategies involve taxes on harmful products such as cigarettes and tax reductions for industries seeking to reduce pollution. Government management of external costs, however, is still in its infancy. Though many ideas have been discussed, few laws have been passed, and these have been haphazardly enforced. In most cases, the fines that have been imposed are too small to force compliance. Economists also point out the dangers of tampering with the cost of goods in a *free market*. Some products will become very expensive, perhaps too expensive to produce at all. Industries may shut down, and jobs may be lost.

The second major failing of GNP has to do not so much with the poisoning of the environment as its exhaustion. GNP takes no account of the depletion of the natural resource base upon which the production of wealth depends. A nation's economy may be working at close to full capacity, creating goods and jobs and a high standard of living, while at the same time it is using up its energy and mineral resources and destroying its forests and soils at rapid rates, achieving short-term gains at the risk of long-term economic catastrophe. This, too, is an external cost, one imposed on future generations who will not be able to maintain the same high standard of living because of depleted stocks of basic materials.

For example, there is considerable uncertainty about how much oil exists in the world, but experts believe that at current rates of consumption proven reserves will last no more than 30 years. New methods to extract oil from shale, tar, and yet-to-be-discovered deposits may provide an additional 40 years' supply. The price for a barrel of crude oil, however, might rise to as high as $90, compared to prices of $20 a barrel today. Coal is more abundant than oil, and existing reserves may last between 60 and 200 years, depending on consumption rates, but the burning of coal puts large amounts of carbon dioxide into the atmosphere, accelerating global warming and unpredictable climate change. Natural gas supplies may last about 60 years. Long before these fossil fuels are completely exhausted, however, they may become too expensive for most energy needs.

When economists measure agricultural production, they fail to account for the overuse and degradation of the land. Each year, worldwide, more than 25 billion tons of topsoil are eroded from prime agricultural land. Each year, 6 million hectares of land are turned into desert (one hectare equals 10,000 square meters, or an area just under three football fields in size). Chemical fertilizers and pesticides, agricultural machinery, and modern irrigation techniques have helped produce bumper crops, but overdependence on such modern agricultural technology has robbed the soil of its resiliency. During the so-called Green Revolution of the past four decades, agricultural production nearly tripled, but today total world grain output has leveled off and is possibly even on the decline.

These trends in natural resource depletion and declining agricultural output show very clearly that environmental degradation may finally be having an adverse effect on economic activity.

THE NEW ECONOMIC THINKING

For these reasons, a number of economists and environmentalists have begun to question the value of GNP and other long-accepted measures of economic growth as meaningful indicators of the quality of life. Some have even questioned the desirability of growth itself. A November 27, 1990, article in the *New York Times* by Peter Passell, headlined "Rebel Economists

The high crop yields of modern agriculture are made possible in part by liberal application of pesticides, but there is a price to pay in terms of poisoned soils and rivers, and these petroleum-based chemicals could become expensive and scarce in the not-too-distant future.

Add Ecological Cost To Price of Progress," described "ecological economists" who "may kindle public debate on some very uncomfortable questions, everything from the need for population control to the compensation owed by the present generation to those who will inherit radioactive reactor waste in the year 3000." Such economists are developing new ways to measure well-being and new definitions of prosperity that try to take into account the state of the environment. They are extending the concept of an economic system to include the natural world in which that system exists. They are insisting that profits and losses be calculated in global terms, and that economies be redesigned to exploit the natural world in balanced ways that preserve something for future generations.

In 1972, economists William Nordhaus and James Tobin began to develop a measurement that came to be called NEW, or *net economic welfare*. Based on GNP, it made several corrections to GNP in an attempt to more accurately measure how productivity contributes to an improved standard of living.

Nordhaus and Tobin added to GNP an estimate for the value
of unpaid labor. They also made an addition for the value of
leisure time. Leisure time is considered invaluable by most
people, but traditional economists cannot measure it as anything
but nonproductive idleness. Most important, Nordhaus and Tobin
made a *subtraction* from GNP for both the cost of urban con-
gestion and the cost of environmental damage. With these
adjustments, the rate of growth of NEW in the United States
since World War II is only half that of GNP. However, NEW has
not become popular with economists, who feel that some of its
adjustments are vague and difficult to quantify. Just how valuable
is a day of leisure time? How valuable is the loss of parkland to
people not yet born?

In 1989, economists at the World Resources Institute, led
by Robert Repetto, went a step further by creating the concept of
GSP, or *gross sustainable productivity*, in which a subtraction was
made from GNP for the depletion of natural resources. Just as
worn-out equipment must be subtracted from new investment to
measure the actual increase in capital goods, Repetto's team
made an allowance for "natural capital depreciation" when they
recalculated national wealth. The new measurement was tested
on the economic performance of Indonesia during the period
from 1971 to 1984, when the country was claiming a remarkable
7% annual rate of economic growth, achieved in large part by
overharvesting its oil and timber reserves. When Repetto's group
deducted the cost of deforestation, soil erosion, and depletion of
oil, they calculated Indonesia's growth rate at a more modest 4%.

Other indicators have appeared that either downgrade or
completely dispense with GNP as a useful measure. In the late
1970s, the Overseas Development Council introduced the PQLI,

or *physical quality of life indicator*, which considers only three factors: life expectancy, infant mortality, and literacy. The *human suffering index* devised by the Population Crisis Committee does include GNP measurements but sets them against measures of inflation, literacy, energy consumption, urbanization, food sufficiency, availability of clean water, and the degree of political freedom. Norman Myers, writing in *Gaia: An Atlas of Planet Management*, mentions primary school enrollment, adequate housing, social welfare protection, and employment as additional measures of real economic progress.

Other economists, concerned about natural resource depletion, have decided that the problem is not simply one of lower real growth rates but of *unsustainable* growth rates. Non-renewable resources or wastefully used renewable resources will eventually disappear, bringing to a complete halt the economic activity that they support. In the case of Indonesia, for example,

Economist Robert Repetto of the World Resources Institute, who developed the concept of gross sustainable productivity, a measure of economic growth that tries to take account of a society's destruction of its natural resources.

the 3% downward adjustment in the growth rate portrays a country that is mortgaging its future for quick economic gain. When all the trees have been cut down and sold for timber, and the hills denuded of tropical forest and their soils washed away, and the last barrel of oil is pumped out of the ground, Indonesia will have no source of income to finance its industrialization, to buy the products and technology of the more developed nations, and to pay back development loans. Unless Indonesia has planned wisely and developed other means of generating wealth, it can look forward to a future of inescapable poverty and underdevelopment.

In the late 1960s, the distinguished economist and social thinker Kenneth E. Boulding was the first to suggest that the global economy have *sustainability*, not unrestrained growth, as its goal. A civilization that hopes to *last*, to pass on real wealth and progress to future generations, cannot take from nature more than it is capable of putting back. Boulding has proposed two indicators: one measuring the total value of disposable goods and those produced by resource depletion, the other measuring the total value of recycled goods and those produced with no net loss to the resource base. The health of an economy would be measured by increases in sustainable production over wasreful production.

In 1977, Herman Daly, senior environmental economist at the World Bank, introduced the idea of the *steady-state economy*. Such an economy, Daly said, should try to *minimize* GNP growth, for the size of GNP is simply a measure of how quickly an economy converts resources into waste in the form of disposable products. Over time, new knowledge and technologies would enable a steady-state economy to expand, but the obsession with growth—in terms of simply producing greater and greater quantities of material goods year after year—would come to an end. For Daly, the obsession with growth is a way to avoid dealing with the problem of distributing wealth fairly among classes and nations, for as long as there will be more of everything tomorrow, it is not as important that some have less today.

And so economists—a few at any rate—have come full circle, from a commitment to unrestrained growth as the best sign of a healthy economy to a recognition that this kind of growth is destructive in the long term. Is the only alternative to growth a world of limits? The steady-state economy would have to strictly regulate the size of its population. It would have political institutions to control resource use and the kinds of goods produced. It would set minimum and maximum levels for personal income. There would be many restrictions on entrepreneurship, and the costs of doing business would be determined in new ways. The steady state economy would in fact be very different from the free market economy that dominates the world today, and to some people it would seem much less free. But it would be a sustainable system, and it would protect future generations from the wastefulness of those who came before them. Whether its advantages outweigh its disadvantages can only be determined through a more complete examination of the way that economic activity affects the environment and the way that environmental problems affect economic activity.

The face of hunger is never easy to look at. This Ethiopian mother and child rest at a refugee camp, awaiting emergency food aid.

chapter 2

THE MEASURE OF OUR FAILURE

In 1990, the gross national product of the entire world was approximately $15 trillion. Of course, this number says very little about the actual wealth and well being of individuals in any particular place. In fact, when this number is broken down and examined more closely, it reveals disturbing patterns of inequality between peoples and nations. In spite of enormous productive capacity, the world seems a place of widespread scarcity rather than abundance and of great imbalances in ownership and control of wealth, land, and power. Poverty, hunger, and preventable disease are common. Though the world economy grew rapidly in the first three decades after World War II—providing people in the industrialized nations with a lavish, consumerist life-style—through the 1970s and 1980s there were growing signs of stagnation and of a looming global economic crisis, brought on in part by environmental degradation.

There is a great disparity between "have" and "have-not" nations. Just three countries—the United States, Japan, and Germany—account for more than half the world's productive output. No other country generates a GNP above the $1 trillion mark. Of more than 200 nations all told, just 10, home to about 25% of the world's population, claim 80% of the world's wealth. With a few exceptions, the richest nations are the industrialized states of the northern hemisphere, and the poorest nations are located on the continents of South America, Africa, and Asia. The richest 10 nations use 75% of the world's energy and 72% of its manufactured steel. The United States alone, home to only 5% of the world's population, uses 25% of the world's energy output. The average American citizen uses more than 12 times as much energy as a citizen of an underdeveloped nation.

What this means for individuals becomes clearer when gross national product is divided by population to obtain per capita GNP. In 1987, the average annual income of a citizen of a developing nation was $670. In 35 of the poorest nations, all of them in Africa and Asia and with a combined population of 2 billion people, per capita GNP was less than $400 a year. By contrast, average income that year in the industrialized nations was $12,070. By 1990, per capita income in the United States had risen to over $19,000 a year, and Japan, Switzerland, and Norway have annual per capita incomes in excess of $20,000.

The already wide gap between rich and poor is growing ever wider. In the two decades between 1965 and 1985, the wealthiest nations increased the average income of their citizens by $3,900. In the same period, the poorest nations were only able to manage a $50 increase. Since 1985, per capita incomes have declined by 10% in Latin America and by 15% in Africa. From 1970 to 1980 the average income of a citizen of Ghana, in West Africa, fell by 30%. Between 1980 and 1990, six more countries sank from the World Bank's "middle income" classification into its "low income" classification. There are exceptions, of course, in the fast-growing economies of East Asia—Japan, Hong Kong, Taiwan, Korea, and Singapore—but for most of the world the 1980s were a period of stagnant or declining growth rates and incomes.

Because per capita GNP is an average, calculated by dividing wealth equally between all the citizens of a nation, it can be misleading as an economic measurement of any specific individual's quality of life, for such an equal division of wealth would be hard to find anywhere in the world. In the United States, the richest 20% of the population receives 44% of the national income, whereas the poorest 20% receives less than 5%. The situation within underdeveloped nations is much more severe. Almost 70% of the population earns less than the average per capita GNP. In Latin America, where land ownership is an important indicator of wealth, 7% of the population controls 93% of the land. In Brazil, the richest 20% of the population receives 64% of the national income, while the poorest 20% receives less than 5%. The real incomes of the poor are much lower than national averages would indicate, and their numbers are much greater.

POVERTY AND ITS CONSEQUENCES

Nearly 1 billion people—one out of every five human beings—live in a state of absolute poverty, unable to obtain enough food to satisfy basic nutritional requirements. About 85% of these people live in Africa and Asia, and about 65% of them are under 15 years of age. About 50% of them are farmers and their families, and another 20% are landless peasants. The average citizen of a developing country consumes only 60% of the calories and 50% of the protein that a citizen of an industrialized country consumes. In some industrialized nations, pets eat more meat than do the people in developing nations.

An inadequate diet stunts growth and mental development, reduces the capacity to work, and increases a person's vulnerability to disease. Even a brief period of ill health can be a catastrophe for a poor family, driving them into debt or forcing them to sell their land, farming implements, or animals. People who do not receive adequate diets are slowly dying; each year

This Bangladeshi woman tries to get clean drinking water from a well damaged by flooding. Throughout the Third World, contaminated drinking water spreads many diseases and kills millions of children every year.

more than 40 million people die from hunger and hunger-related diseases. Nearly 15 million of them are children.

Almost 1.5 billion of the world's people lack safe drinking water and proper sanitation and sewage facilities, which has devastating consequences for their health, as a number of different disease organisms thrive in polluted water. About 200 million human beings suffer from schistosomiasis, a serious intestinal infection spread by freshwater snails. About 500 million suffer from trachoma, an eye infection and the leading cause of blindness. Every year, 6 million people die of diarrhea and 3 million die of tuberculosis. Millions more succumb to malaria, hookworm, yellow fever, cholera, typhoid, dysentery, and hepatitis—all preventable or treatable diseases arising from poor living conditions. Yet, according to the United Nation's Children's Fund (UNICEF), fewer than 20% of the world's children are immunized against such diseases. Whereas the average life expectancy for an American is 75 years, for an African it is only 52 years. The infant mortality rate in the United States is less than 10 deaths per thousand births; in Africa it is more than 100 deaths per thousand births. Approximately 500,000 women die in pregnancy and childbirth every year. In the underdeveloped world only one in nine people lives within walking distance of a medical facility, and there is, on average, only one doctor for every 14,000 people. In war-torn and famine-stricken Ethiopia, there is only one doctor for every 77,000 people.

Poverty and hunger make it harder to educate people. About 25% of the world's adults—nearly all of them in the underdeveloped world and two-thirds of them women—are illiterate. Africa, where three out of every four people are unable to read, suffers the most in this respect. The children of the poor must either work or help to raise siblings while their parents work and are thus often unable to attend school regularly. In Calcutta, India, 60% of school-age children do not receive primary education for these reasons. According to UNICEF, of the 100 million six-year-olds who in 1990 entered primary school in underdeveloped countries, 40 million will drop out. Without education, individuals find it difficult to secure anything but the most unskilled and lowest paying jobs, which reinforces their poverty. People who cannot read or write are often ignorant of their legal and political rights and are more likely to be exploited by the wealthy and the powerful. Studies have consistently shown that education is one of the most effective long-term economic investments a society can make, one that yields numerous benefits when educated children grow up and enter the work force. Failure to educate today's generation is a fairly reliable indicator that a nation will be at an enormous disadvantage twenty years from now.

AFFLUENCE AT A PRICE

If life in the underdeveloped nations is often short and brutal, have the citizens of the industrialized nations, with their extravagant use of energy and natural resources, achieved paradise? Certainly the developed world has greater wealth, a higher standard of living and physical comfort, and hardly anyone there starves to death. But unemployment and poverty persist in spite of economic growth. In 1991, one out of every ten Americans was receiving food stamps, an income supplement for the purchase of nutritional necessities. Even in the developed world, prosperity is not enjoyed by everyone.

Whereas treatable common infectious diseases, made worse by poor nutrition, are the great scourge of poor nations, the people of the rich nations suffer the effects of a different kind of malnutrition—overconsumption of unhealthy high-fat, high-sugar, low-fiber foods. As a result, citizens of affluent nations have high rates of obesity, heart disease, hypertension, stroke, cancer, diabetes, and kidney failure. Strokes and heart attacks are now responsible for more than 50% of all deaths in the rich nations. A different life-style and diet would prevent much of this illness, but left untreated, such diseases ultimately require expensive medical intervention, raising health costs. Widespread drug and alcohol abuse and cigarette smoking only make matters worse. Nervous disorders, stress, and insecurity about the future seem an inseparable part of the high-tech, fast-paced, growth-oriented life-style of the richer countries. Industrialized nations spend more on tranquilizers than the entire health budget of more than 60 of the poorest nations.

In spite of these many problems, it is undeniable that most citizens of the industrialized nations are more affluent, enjoy a more comfortable way of life, and are more economically secure than their counterparts in the underdeveloped nations. But can the industrialized nations sustain this affluence?

If it is based, as at present, on the rapid exhaustion of natural resources and the fouling of the environment with unacceptable levels of waste and poison, then the answer is no, for rapid and uncontrolled economic growth is precipitating a global environmental crisis of unprecedented proportions. Intensive agriculture—farming that depends on large inputs of fertilizers and pesticides derived from petrochemicals, oil to run mechanical planting and harvesting equipment, and artificial irrigation—is proving to be unsustainable. Worldwide, the amount of acreage planted with basic grains is decreasing as billions of tons of fertile topsoil erode away and groundwater supplies are drained dry by modern farming practices. Deforestation threatens many species with extinction and contributes to soil erosion as well as floods, droughts, and global climate change. Air pollutants also threaten to bring about climate change, not to mention more forest and crop devastation through the creation of acid rain. Exotic industrial chemicals threaten the ozone layer that regulates the inflow of harmful solar radiation. The hazardous wastes created by industry are dangerous to human health and are costly to dispose of. Each year, the United States alone generates 260 million tons of toxic wastes.

Of course, the most controversial question affecting all nations is how long cheap energy will be available. Proven oil reserves should last another 30 to 40 years at mid-1980s rates of consumption; reserves of natural gas, at least another 60 years. The rate of consumption, however, increases every year as populations grow and newly industrialized countries claim a greater share of energy resources. Coal reserves could last for more than another 200 years, but the burning of coal may create unacceptable levels of air pollution, acid rain, and gases that promote global warming. There are presently over 400 nuclear power plants throughout the world supplying about 5% of its total energy needs, but when the costs of safe containment and safe disposal of radioactive waste are considered, nuclear power is not proving as economical or manageable as had been hoped. Almost

2 billion of the world's people depend upon the collection of ordinary fuelwood for cooking, heating, and other energy needs, and deforestation threatens this essential human resource. There seems good reason to worry about the future availability of energy.

However, almost every previous prediction of energy catastrophe has proved wrong. The history of energy is the history of the discovery of new reserves, the discovery of economical substitutes for existing energy sources, and the discovery of new, more potent energy technologies—from wood to coal to oil to plutonium. Indeed, some analysts deny that there is any energy crisis. They assert that there are no practical limits to supplying all the energy the world needs and therefore no need to worry about economic growth in this regard. In *Population Matters*, Julian L. Simon concludes, "A look at the statistical history of energy supplies shows that the trend has been toward plenty rather than toward scarcity. . . . From these data we may conclude with considerable confidence that energy will be less costly and more available in the future than in the past." Those who agree with Simon place great faith in technological innovation to provide continuous solutions to the energy problem and generally look with favor upon nuclear power, in spite of its drawbacks.

Even though all past doomsday predictions have proved false, and even if the discovery of new energy reserves and new technologies push back depletion schedules by decades, there is something vaguely disturbing about this line of reasoning, what E. F. Schumacher in *Small Is Beautiful* calls "limitless optimism." Most scientists would agree that the earth's resources are finite— they exist in fixed, limited amounts. It is true that the earth is not a closed energy system. It receives energy from the sun every day and radiates some of that energy back into space. But the time

Economist Julian L. Simon has studied the history of energy prices and believes that technological innovation will continue to make sufficient energy available at a reasonable cost in the future, despite the claims of environmentalists.

scale on which basic energy resources, such as coal and oil and natural gas, are created is much longer than the time scale on which modern industrial society uses up those resources.

The laws of physics state that energy cannot be recycled. Energy is lost when it is used, usually as it is transformed into heat that dissipates and cannot be recaptured. So whereas any particular prediction of resource exhaustion may be proven false, in the long run, at current unsustainable rates of consumption, the world *will* exhaust its energy reserves. Not only energy, but the soil itself—the nutrient-rich material that produces human food—can be degraded or washed away faster than natural processes of weathering and erosion can recreate it. Environmentalists may not have been very successful—so far—in pinpointing exact dates of resource depletion, but when they study *rates* of depletion, the conclusion is inescapable: the global industrial engine, as it now operates, cannot continue to run indefinitely.

And what of the poor nations, which are home to most of the world's people and are apportioned so little of its resources? Are present imbalances to continue until the industrialized nations consume the last reserves of oil and gas and coal? Or should there be a massive transfer of wealth, technology, and industrial capacity from the rich nations to the poor nations? To raise the living standards of citizens in the underdeveloped world, there will have to be a wrenching shift in access to remaining energy resources, and the rich nations will have to exercise restraint in pursuing economic growth and practice efficiency and conservation in resource use.

What claims do underdeveloped nations have on these resources? By what right can they demand a larger share of the wealth? What are the consequences for the rich nations if this redistribution of global resources does not take place? How are rich and poor nations tied together, historically and econom- cally? How do these relationships affect the global environment? These questions will be examined in the next chapter.

As rural unemployment and poverty grow throughout the Third World, the poor migrate to the cities, where they live in shantytowns such as this one on the outskirts of Rio de Janeiro, Brazil.

T H E   T H I R D   W O R L D

The term *Third World* comes from the French *le tiers monde* and was first used in the 1950s as a descriptive term for those newly independent but poor nations that had freed themselves from colonial rule by the European powers after World War II. Many of these nations considered themselves politically nonaligned with either the free market economies of the so-called First World or the centrally planned economies of the Second World.

Political analysts today use many terms to describe these countries—"less advanced," "underdeveloped," "developing," or "less developed countries (LDCs)." Most recently, the fashion has been to call them the countries of "the South," from the observation that, in general, the poorer countries are to be found in the southern hemisphere. Whatever the terminology, there exists a large group of nations that share a common heritage of colonial exploitation and poverty and are still experiencing tremendous obstacles to their economic development even after decades of independence. These countries often respond to their predicament by destroying their environments and overexploiting their natural resources in order to ensure their short-term survival.

THE PATTERN OF
UNDERDEVELOPMENT

The reasons for the profound differences in rates of
economic development between rich and poor nations are
debated by historians and involve many geographical and cultural
factors. It must be remembered, however, that there were great
civilizations in what are today some of the poorest regions of the
world hundreds and even thousands of years before the peoples
of Europe possessed a written language or knowledge of
agriculture.

During the 15th and 16th centuries in Europe, a rebirth
of scientific inquiry was accompanied by a new spirit of ac-
quisitiveness. Aggressive mercantile states—supported by new
classes of traders, primitive manufacturers, knights turned
explorers and soldiers of fortune, and city folk with a new taste for
luxuries—were seized by a strong expansionist impulse. At this
critical point in its history, Europe was able to make enormous
practical advances in the sciences of geography, navigation,
shipbuilding, and military technology and organization, which
enabled it to fulfill its need for raw materials, natural resources,
and luxury items by means of overseas expeditions of explora-
tion, trade, conquest, and settlement.

Tentatively at first, with small groups of adventurers,
merchants, and missionaries, but finally with large modern armies
and all the civil apparatus necessary for political control, the
Europeans ventured into Africa, Asia, and the Americas. They
spent the 16th through the 19th centuries conquering, colonizing,
and extracting the wealth of new territories. The great Spanish

empire of the 16th century was built with the gold and silver brought back from Central and South America. Great Britain achieved similar conquests in North America, western and southern Africa, the Middle East, India, and other parts of Asia. Portugal took the territory that is now Brazil as well as Angola and Mozambique in Africa and part of India. France claimed Madagascar, Gabon, Morocco, Algeria—all in Africa—and Indochina. Italy took Libya and parts of Somalia, and Germany claimed Cameroon, Namibia, and Tanzania. Even tiny Belgium took what is now Zaire, and the Netherlands took Indonesia. In *The Rise and Fall of the Great Powers*, Paul Kennedy states that, "In the year 1800, Europeans occupied or controlled 35 percent of the land surface of the world; by 1878 this figure had risen to 67 percent, and by 1914 to over 84 percent." The ultimate exploitation occurred from the 16th through the 19th centuries, when Europeans enslaved and traded in human beings, transporting Africans by the millions to work on the farms, fields, and plantations of the New World.

The tactics of conquest and control were varied and clever. By the time the nations of Europe consolidated their empires at the end of the 19th century, they enjoyed overwhelming advantages over their colonial dominions. Their economies were based on the irresistible power of modern machine industry. Technology applied to mass communication enabled these governments to mold public opinion and inspire a sense of national purpose based on notions of national and racial superiority. The Europeans possessed modern weapons, well-equipped armies, and a willingness to use brute force to further their political objectives. The relationship between conqueror and conquered was perhaps best expressed by the British poet Hilaire Belloc, who, with a reference to Sir Hiram Stevens Maxim, inventor in 1884 of the first fully automatic machine gun, wrote of colonized peoples:

> Whatever happens, we have got
> The Maxim gun, and they have not.

The Europeans extolled the virtues of their rule and spoke endlessly of the economic, social, legal, and moral progress their governance would bring. However, in most cases the economic development of the colonies followed a one-sided and predictable path. In the interior of the country, mines, farms, and plantations were established to extract valuable minerals—gold, diamonds, metal ores—or to grow valued tropical products—tea, coffee, cotton, sugar, rubber, fruits, and spices. Roads and railroads were built to move these raw materials from the interior to coastal areas. Cities grew up around the seaports and way stations as administrative and warehousing centers for the activity of extraction. The ruling powers generally exhibited little interest in the economic or social development of the territories they ruled. The entire economic and governmental system was geared toward arranging for the export of the desired goods and materials back to Europe, not toward local economic development or for improving the welfare of indigenous peoples.

In order to create the labor force for these mines and farms, it was necessary to destroy the self-sufficiency of the conquered peoples—to take away their land and destroy traditional economic activity. Formerly independent farmers, herders, and hunters became dispossessed and impoverished mine workers and agricultural laborers, dependent upon the new rulers for employment and a cash income to buy the food and necessities they used to produce for themselves. Michael Lofchie of the African Studies Center at the University of California, Los Angeles, states that "the living standard of the peasantry had to be deliberately lowered to the point that wage labor became the only alternative to starvation or utter destitution." In addition to extracting raw materials, the Europeans sought new markets for their manufactured goods in the colonies. To create these markets it was necessary to destroy the competition from native industries and handicraft production. In India, a whole class of spinners and weavers were wiped out because they could not compete with the cheap, machine-made textiles brought in from English factories.

Sometimes the rule of the European power was direct, undisguised, and brutal. At other times the colonizers found it useful to maintain the fiction of local rule by working through some regional king, prince, sheik, sultan, rajah, or chief. Tribal, clan, religious, and class differences were exploited to keep people from uniting and acting against the foreign power. Often, small groups of indigenous people were educated and indoctrinated in European ways and formed a new, native, urban middle class, taking over many of the lesser functions of colonial administration. Such groups enlarged the demand for manufactured goods from European industries. They acted as a buffer between the foreign ruler and the most exploited and were used to prove that the benefits of European civilization would eventually "trickle down" to the colonized. Sharing a few of the benefits of empire with a small, privileged class of indigenous people did not disturb the imperial powers as long as the flow of wealth to the mother country continued.

Such has been the history of most of the countries now considered part of the Third World. For decades, and in some cases for centuries, the economies of these nations were restructured to provide raw materials for European industry. Exploitation and political domination became especially intense after about 1870, when European empires reached a pinnacle of development and self-confidence. Certainly, when one studies the history of Third World nations, there is little reason to ask with astonishment why they are so poor. Activist and author Michael Parenti points out that "the stupendous fortunes that were—and still are being—extracted by the European and North American investors should remind us that there are very few really poor nations in what today is commonly called the Third World. Brazil is rich; Indonesia is rich; and so are the Philippines, Chile, Bolivia, Zaire, Mexico, India, and Malaysia. Only the people are poor. . . . In a word, the Third World is not 'underdeveloped' but overexploited."

AFTER INDEPENDENCE

World War II changed the form, if not the substance, of the relationship between rich and poor nations. In Asia, especially, the vulnerability of the old colonial regimes was made evident as they collapsed before the new Japanese conquerors, and by war's end the ideals of freedom and democracy preached by the victorious powers had been taken to heart by national liberation movements in many of the colonies. Democratic expectations were raised, and by the time peace was concluded in 1945, it was no longer possible for the nations of Europe to reestablish the old colonial system. Weakened by the war and under various internal pressures to reform, the European nations could not sustain the painful and bloody colonial wars they were forced to fight to regain control. In a relatively short period of time—about two decades, all told—and at great cost, the nations of the Third World achieved political independence.

But independence did not magically solve the problems facing these countries. Their economies had been developed to serve the interests of foreign powers. Though Third World nations were rich in natural resources, they often lacked the technological and administrative skills and—most important—the money, the investment capital, to develop new domestic industries and become self-sufficient. They still produced mainly raw materials, which could only be marketed to the industrialized nations, which were powerful enough to set the prices that would be paid for these goods. In turn, many of the simplest manufactured consumer goods had to be purchased from the developed nations, at prices set by them. What the industrialized nations now discovered was that they were able to maintain extremely favorable economic relations with their former colonies—now independent but still poor—without the "expense" of actual political control. This new relationship has been labeled *neocolonialism*.

In the years following independence, some Third World countries struggled desperately to overcome their problems and made significant strides in alleviating poverty, hunger, sickness, and illiteracy, but the initial disadvantages of most of these nations were so great that few could make much progress on their own. Many of these nations also suffered from continuing political instability, sharp internal divisions of wealth, and conflicts between rural poor and urban elites. In too many cases their new governments were undemocratic and used the military and the secret police to protect the interests of a dictator, a ruling junta, or a small privileged class. Desperate to improve their situation, many Third World nations turned to the rich nations of the West for money and a development strategy that would end the cycle of underdevelopment.

The new strategy devised by the economists, bankers, and technocrats of the developed nations called for programs of rapid industrialization, the development of an urban middle class with consumerist habits dependent on imported goods, a politically stable government protected by a strong military, and the conversion of small-scale subsistence agriculture to the large-scale production of export crops—*cash crops*—to give poorer countries something to sell in world markets. This modernization was to be financed by foreign investment and by loans from the banks and lending institutions of the rich nations.

This strategy for growth was developed by economists under the influence of theories of free trade and comparative advantage that suggest that each nation should concentrate on producing those goods it is best able to produce and trade its products with other nations for the commodities it cannot produce efficiently or cheaply. For example, a warm tropical country with a long growing season, plentiful rainfall, the right soils, and cheap rural labor is ideal for growing bananas or coffee or cotton and should grow and sell these products to the industrialized countries, which are better suited to making the tractors, mechanical harvesters, and fertilizers that the tropical country needs for its agricultural products. In theory, everyone trades goods produced under the most advantageous circumstances, earns income to buy from others what they cannot efficiently produce for themselves, and all nations are drawn together into a single, integrated global economy.

In practice, however, such a system has perpetuated the subordinate role of poorer countries as suppliers of raw materials to the rich countries, just as in the colonial period. When these raw materials return to the poorer countries in the form of manufactured or processed goods, they are much more expensive. The result is a pattern of trading relationships in which poor countries pay out more than they take in, and their economies stagnate. Alan B. Durning of the Worldwatch Institute states that "the term developing nation has become a cruel parody: many countries are not so much developing as they are disintegrating." He goes on to quote the Uruguayan historian Eduardo Galeano on the theory of comparative advantage: "The division of labor among nations is that some specialize in winning and others in losing."

Initially, Third World nations financed their development programs by borrowing from other governments and commercial banks, but they have come to depend increasingly on two institutions created by a United Nations conference held at Bretton Woods, New Hampshire, in 1944. These are the International Bank for Reconstruction and Development, commonly known as the World Bank, and the International Monetary Fund, or IMF. The purpose of the World Bank is to make loans to assist economic development, and the purpose of the IMF is to promote world trade. Through these two sister institutions, the rich nations advance huge sums of money that the poor nations can borrow, with the lenders controlling the interest rates and the terms under which the loans are approved. Before the 1970s, when terms

Environmentalists have attacked the World Bank, the International Monetary Fund, and other lending institutions for their financing of projects that promote environmental degradation and for the austerity programs they force on poor nations in an effort to encourage debt repayment.

were still reasonable, the Third World countries went on a borrowing spree.

The problem, it is now clear, is that the borrowed money has been misspent. Only rarely has even a single aspect of the modernization strategy had the desired effect of creating real economic development. Attempts to make over Third World cultures in the image of modern capitalism, to accomplish in two or three decades what it took the Western world 200 years to achieve, have failed in all but a few nations. Policies aimed at promoting a prosperous urban middle class channeled development money to the rich in the cities, and a good deal of this money was squandered on the purchase of luxury items and consumer goods manufactured in the rich nations. The great demand among this class for foreign goods worked *against* economic development by discouraging the growth of competing national industries. Governments anxious for legitimacy overooked the fact that their populations were mainly rural and poor and spent their development money on "prestige" projects—presidential palaces, new office buildings, sports stadiums, highways, hospitals, and modern air-travel terminals—none of which could improve the often desperate conditions in the countryside. President Felix Houphouet-Boigny of the Ivory Coast recently spent $200,000,000 to build a monumental cathedral in the village of Yamasoukro, even though less than 15% of the population of his nation is Catholic and poverty there is widespread. Land formerly used for subsistence farming was set aside for cash crops, resulting in increased poverty in rural areas.

The rich and the powerful also often sent their money abroad instead of investing it locally, sequestering their wealth in foreign banks or investing in foreign property as a hedge against any future political instability in their own countries. By 1987, the upper classes of Latin America had transferred about $250 billion to overseas investments and holdings. The easy flow of development money corrupted ruling elites and led to an orgy of consumption, with little investment in productive enterprises. Susan George of the Transnational Institute, in her compelling book *A Fate Worse Than Debt*, draws a grim portrait of General Mobuto Sese Soko, for 20 years the dictator of Zaire, one of the poorest of the Third World countries. General Mobuto owns nine presidential mansions in his own country, an even larger number of chateaus and estates in Belgium, France, Spain, Italy, and Switzerland, as well as a fleet of ships, planes, and more than 50 Mercedes limousines. Counting his large stock holdings in native agricultural enterprises and foreign corporations, it has been estimated that his net worth equals the national debt of $6 billion. In effect, General Mobuto and his family and supporters have taken for themselves every last dollar loaned to Zaire for development.

Military spending is another part of the problem. Barbara Conable, president of the World Bank, has calculated that poor nations spend about $200 billion a year—20% of all the money they have borrowed—on arms purchases. Ethiopia spends twice as much on arms as it spends on health and education combined. Before it was replaced by a democratically elected government in 1983, the military junta of Argentina spent $10 billion, one-fifth of the money loaned to it, on weapons. Up to half of the oil purchased by the poorer nations is earmarked for the military. Military spending, especially when arms are purchased abroad and not manufactured in one's own country, contributes nothing to economic development.

Even the most basic efforts at industrialization have failed, sometimes as a result of corruption, sometimes through honest but foolish investment in ill-conceived megaprojects, and sometimes because of sheer fascination with expensive but inappropriate Western technology. In their rush to imitate the industrial vitality of the rich nations, Third World governments invested heavily in expanding their energy-generating capacity, sometimes with catastrophic results. In 1976, Ferdinand Marcos of the Philippines gave $2.1 billion in borrowed money to the

Westinghouse corporation to build a nuclear power plant in the province of Luzon on the island of Bataan. Marcos himself was reported to have received $80 million in "commissions" through his agents, but the power plant was built in an earthquake zone next to an active volcano. Corazon Aquino, Marcos's democratically elected successor as president of the Philippines, wisely refused to allow the plant to operate.

Egypt's Aswan High Dam on the upper Nile, built between 1960 and 1970, was supposed to provide cheap electricity for the nation. But the dam has restricted the flow of water, silt, and nutrients that used to flood the lower river valley and make the soil fertile. Now much of the dam's hydroelectric power is consumed by chemical plants producing artificial fertilizers to do what the river once did by itself. A series of expensive

In the underdeveloped nations, large dams and hydroelectric projects provide cheap energy and irrigation water but often flood rainforests, divert rivers, promote waterborne diseases, and force into debt the governments that borrowed money to build them.

hydroelectric projects in Brazil have dammed tributaries of the Amazon and flooded thousands of hectares of rainforest, but the dams are not likely to provide as much electricity as hoped. Heavy sediment in Amazonian rivers reduces the efficiency and useful life of the turbines. Throughout the Third World, the diversion of rivers to meet the needs of ambitious hydroelectric projects has destroyed towns and villages, displaced hundreds of thousands of people, and increased the risk of illness from waterborne diseases.

DEBT AND THE ENVIRONMENT

The end result of all this borrowing has been that the developing nations of the world have acquired a crushing burden of debt. The poor nations now owe the industrialized nations more than $1.3 trillion. In the early 1980s, the developing nations were receiving a net inflow of about $40 billion a year from the developed nations. But after 1988, interest payments on these loans had grown so large that the poor nations now annually pay the rich nations $30 billion more than they receive in new aid. The ironic result of the various grand schemes for modernization of the past several decades is that there is now a net transfer of wealth from poor nations to the rich nations, and the gap between rich and poor nations is growing even wider.

Brazil, which in 1989 owed $113 billion, is the Third World's largest debtor nation. Mexico, with a debt of $103 billion, is second. In 1982, Mexico threatened to *default*—to declare its inability to continue making payments on what it owed. This almost precipitated an international financial crisis, until the lending countries gave Mexico even more money and *rescheduled* its debt—reduced the required rate of repayment.

As more and more governments face the prospect of being unable to pay their debts, the World Bank and the IMF intervene with "adjustment" schemes. The debt is rescheduled and more money is lent, but the debtor nations are forced to adopt austerity programs that require their governments to reduce public spending and do everything possible to increase

Net resource transfers to developing countries, 1973 to 1987

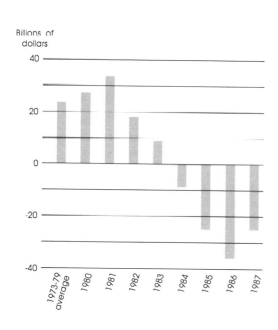

As the graph shows, since the early 1980s the developing nations have been paying out to the industrialized nations about 30 billion dollars more than they receive in new loans and grants. This drain on national income makes investment in economic growth difficult.

(Adapted from *World Development Report 1988* for the World Bank by Oxford University Press)

exports to raise money for repayment, which often results in even greater impoverishment as expenditures for health, education, and rural development decline, leading to increased unemployment, malnutrition, sickness, and illiteracy. Another measure forced on developing nations by their creditors is currency devaluation. Existing money is replaced by new money that is worth less, or governments enforce price increases on basic goods—food, gasoline, electricity—while holding wages at existing levels, which reduces living standards.

For most Third World nations, the production of exports has not brought in as much money as anticipated because there are too many nations trying to sell the same products in the same international markets. The pattern of colonial development left many countries with only one or two products to sell—raw materials such as iron ore, tin, copper, rubber, or agricultural products such as sugar, coffee, cocoa, rice, and cotton. In the 1980s, as overall demand from the developed nations dropped as the result of recession and slow growth rates, the world marketplace became glutted with these products, and the overall price of such exports dropped 40%.

The environmental consequences of the Third World's debt crisis have been catastrophic. Obligated to manage their economies according to the dictates of the World Bank and the IMF, Third World nations have responded to the debt crisis in the only way they know how—by selling whatever they can to raise cash. The result is often the frenzied and thoughtless harvesting of natural resources and consequent grave damage to the environment—the scenario primarily responsible, for example, for the destruction of Indonesia's rainforests at the rate of 2 million acres a year. Though the sale of tropical timber brings developing nations about $8 billion annually, the cost of deforestation, in terms of droughts, soil erosion, displacement of indigenous peoples, loss of species, and worldwide climate change is immeasurable. In November 1991, the people of the Philippines paid a terrible price for years of deforestation when a devastating flood killed 2,000 people. Approximately 80% of the original forests of the Philippines have now disappeared, principally to supply wood to Japan for the home construction industry and for *waribashi*, the 20 billion pairs of disposable wooden chopsticks the Japanese use every year.

Many analysts now believe that the austerity programs put into effect by governments desperate to pay off their debts only increase regional poverty, and poverty pushes people to destroy their environment. "The cruel logic of short-term needs," says Alan B. Durning of the Worldwatch Institute, "forces landless families to raze plots in the rain forest, plow steep slopes, and shorten fallow periods. Ecological decline, in turn, perpetuates poverty, as degraded ecosystems offer diminishing yields to their poor inhabitants. A self-feeding downward spiral of economic deprivation and ecological degradation takes hold."

Susan George in *The Debt Boomerang* points out that the most indebted Third World nations—Brazil, Mexico, India, Indonesia, Nigeria, Venezuela, the Philippines, and Thailand— are also the nations that are most rapidly destroying their tropical forests. The connection between debt and deforestation is hard to deny, and George concludes that "The 'export-led growth' model, on which the Fund [the IMF] and the World Bank insist, is a purely extractive one involving more the 'mining' than the management—much less the conservation—of resources."

Home to the most extensive rainforests in the world, Brazil presents a classic case of economic shortsightedness and environmental destruction. In northeast Brazil, the over-concentration of land ownership in the form of huge estates and plantations has traditionally left large numbers of the population landless and unemployed, despite the presence of abundant agricultural resources. Uninterested in implementing meaningful land reform, Brazil's government has instead encouraged this "excess" population to push into, clear, and colonize the vast, unexplored lands of Amazonia to the west.

The pattern of destruction documented in the Amazonian state of Rondônia by the British environmental activist Adrian Cowell in his book *The Decade of Destruction* has come to be the rule in the Brazilian rainforest. In Rondônia, the government built a road, BR364, from Pôrto Velho into the heart of the forest and enticed settlers with land grants. The settlers, who slashed and burned areas of rainforest to grow food, soon found themselves at war with the Uru Eu Wau Wau Indians for control of the land. Routed by guns and communicable diseases, the Indians retreated deeper into the forest. But the soils of Amazonia are poor in nutrients and often give out after three or four growing seasons; the settlers, left with deeds to worthless land, push deeper into the jungle as well, clearing more land ahead of them and resuming their war with the Indians. Behind the settlers come wealthy cattle ranchers with tax incentives from the government to produce beef for export; the land cleared, used, exhausted, and then deserted by the settlers is now used for grazing cattle. Where the settlers do not move off the land quickly enough to suit the ranchers, they are driven off by hired gunmen.

In successive waves of colonization, first the poor and then the rich move across the Amazon, consuming it for short-term gain. In the end the Indians are driven out or killed, the poor are still landless and without means of support, and the ranchers have reaped a quick profit and are ready to ravage more of the vast forest, leaving behind them worthless, degraded land. The colonization of Rondônia, known as the Polonoreste project, was encouraged by the Brazilian government to earn money from the sale of beef to North America and Europe, and it was approved and financed by the World Bank. Unfortunately, the export of beef has not proved to be an effective way to earn foreign exchange, and the only ones to profit from the venture—and others like it—have been the wealthy ranchers, while Brazil's poor, as well as its unique ecosystems, have suffered. Talking about another region of Amazonia, Cary Fowler and Pat Mooney in their book *Shattering* report that "In recent years only forty-four thousand dollars in beef has been exported annually from the state of Pará, for example, compared to thirty-three million dollars in Brazil nuts."

THE WORLD CRISIS

And so, after nearly five decades of export-oriented economic "development," both industrialized and under-developed countries find themselves locked together in an impossible situation. Speaking of only one continent's debt problems, Jackie Roddick in *Dance of the Millions* points out that "The burden on Latin America is more than double the level of post–First World War reparations imposed on Germany at the

Treaty of Versailles and widely held to be a major factor in the tensions contributing to the rise of Hitler." In spite of the vast sums of money spent by their governments, the people of the Third World grow poorer, their remaining natural resources are sold off, and their environment is degraded. Producing for export—to pay off foreign debt—rather than for local consumption magnifies the problems of hunger and overpopulation, yet there seems to be no way that Third World nations can enter the world market on equitable terms.

Whenever a Third World nation tries to extract itself from the cycle of indebtedness and adopt a self-sustaining development program, it meets hostility from the industrialized nations and their banks, whose main goal is not development but a steady flow of interest payments to maintain their own solvency. When Alan Garcia was elected president of Peru in 1985, he was faced with a national debt of $16 billion and quickly announced that he would limit the rate of repayment of that debt to no more than 10% of Peru's earnings from exports. In 1986, the IMF refused to endorse any additional loans for Peru, and other banks followed its lead. As a result, Peru's rate of economic growth had fallen by 20% by 1989, and unemployment and poverty increased drastically. In 1990, the new Peruvian president, Alberto Fujimori, reversed his predecessor's policy and instituted an austerity program to raise cash to pay back the debt more quickly. Prices for food, water, and gasoline were raised, and many more Peruvians sank into poverty. Increasing the cost of clean water was especially tragic, for now a cholera epidemic rages in Peru and threatens to spread throughout South America.

Even attacking the emphasis on export-oriented agriculture brings problems for Third World governments. In 1992,

President Robert Mugabe of Zimbabwe raised the possibility of expropriating the large estates still owned by white farmers in his country and distributing the land to impoverished black agricultural workers. This would not only redistribute land but also alter its use, reducing production of export crops and increasing production of food for local consumption. Though many more people would be productively employed on these smaller plots, export income would fall, repayment of foreign debt would slow, and to some extent Zimbabwe would withdraw from the global economy. Predictably, Western governments and lending institutions have protested Mugabe's plan. Third World countries that try to steer their economies away from development programs based on debt repayment find themselves isolated and under enormous economic stress. Consequently, there is a great temptation to succumb to development programs planned by the industrialized nations.

The debt that Third World nations have incurred is unlikely ever to be repaid, yet the lender nations have little choice but to keep on rescheduling the loans, for a default could mean the collapse of the international banking system and a worldwide depression of unprecedented magnitude. The day of economic and environmental reckoning is thus pushed farther into the future, but, inevitably, it will arrive.

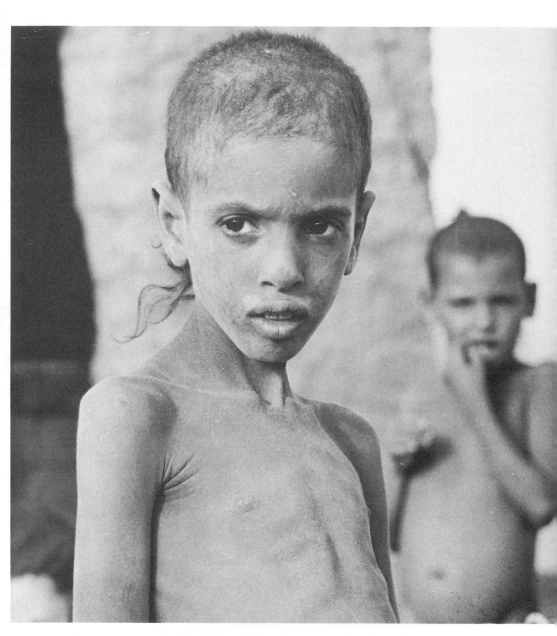

Every year, nearly 15 million children in poor nations die of hunger and hunger-related diseases.

chapter 4

F O O D

The most fundamental economic question concerning food is: why is there hunger? Why are one billion people unable to obtain enough food to satisfy their basic nutritional needs? Is it simply because there too many people to feed, or are the causes more complex?

The world depends on three sources of food—plants and agricultural products, meat and animal products, and food from the sea. Two of these sources are derivative. Most animals depend on plants for their food, and marine creatures feed on abundant surface-dwelling, single-celled, photosynthetic plants called phytoplankton. Green plants turn the sun's energy into food, and green plants ultimately nourish all the other creatures of the earth.

Only about 11% of the world's total land area—1.5 billion hectares—is given over to the cultivation of crops. Though agricultural experts believe that it might be possible to double the land area under cultivation, there are limiting factors—the cost of fertilizers, pesticides, machinery, and the availability of water. About 30 different crops are grown on this land; four of them— wheat, corn, rice, and potatoes—constitute more than half of the world's total agricultural production. Other important basic food crops include barley, oats, rye, sorghum, millet, cassava, and soybean.

Approximately twice the land area devoted to agriculture serves as pastureland for grazing animals. There are about 10 billion domesticated animals on the planet, two for every single human being. They provide meat, milk, cheese, materials for clothing, and draft power in nonindustrialized countries. High-protein food is supplied by about a dozen species of cattle, sheep, goats, pigs, chickens, turkeys, geese, and ducks.

There is considerable debate over whether animal husbandry is an efficient way to produce food for a world of hungry people. As one moves up the food chain, energy is lost. For example, it takes about 10 calories' worth of grain to produce 1 calorie of steak, and about 40% of the world's grains are used to feed livestock. Might it not be better to reduce the size of the herds and use the grain to feed people directly, both increasing the food supply and reducing consumption of unhealthy, high-fat foods? The Global Tomorrow Coalition states that "Of the various forms of animal protein, grain-fed beef is the most inefficient to produce, requiring about 16 pounds of grain and soybeans to produce a pound of beef. . . . The greater the human consumption of animal products, the fewer people can be fed." But ranchers are quick to point out that many types of livestock are not grain-fed but graze the grass and shrubs on land that is unsuitable for cultivation. Such animals are not in competition with human beings for food crops. A 1990 fact sheet from the National Cattlemen's Association states that "Only through ruminant (four-stomach) grazing animals can we harvest food from the more than 1 billion acres of range and pastureland in the U.S. At least 85% of the grazing land is too high, too rough, too dry or too wet to grow cultivated crops. . . . The U.S. has more than enough cropland to grow both feed grains and food crops. In fact, because of grain surpluses, government crop programs involve removal of land from grain production."

This is true in the United States, but in many poorer countries cropland *is* in short supply, and the conflict between beef production for export and staple food production is a real one. With so much of the world's grain supply fed to livestock in underdeveloped countries, fewer people are fed than might be. "While an acre of land devoted to corn and sorghum can produce over 1,200 pounds of grain a year," state Frances Moore Lappé and Joseph Collins, "that same land devoted to cattle ranching barely yields 50 pounds of meat."

As a percentage of total food intake, the ocean harvest is the world's least important food source, but it provides humans with between 20% and 90% of the animal protein in their diets, depending upon where they live. Some of this protein comes to

In Argentina, cattle are herded into a Buenos Aires slaughterhouse. In many Latin American countries, using the best land to produce beef for export decreases the amount of land available for local food production.

people indirectly, in the form of fish meal added to livestock feed or even to fertilizer. With the exception of whales and large marine mammals, there are four main groups of ocean creatures taken for food. Demersal, or bottom-dwelling, fish include cod, haddock, and sole. Pelagic, or surface-dwelling, fish include herring, mackerel, tuna, salmon, and anchovy and are by far the largest group of fish harvested. Crustaceans, or shellfish, include lobster, crab, and shrimp. Cephalopods and mollusks, such as octopus, squid, oysters, and clams, are a small but important part of some people's diets.

Since 1950, new fishing technologies and well-equipped long-range fishing fleets have increased the ocean catch by more than 300%, but in recent years fish stocks have been declining. In the North Atlantic, there has been a 90% decline in the catch of haddock, cod, and halibut. During the 1970s, the herring catch in the North Sea fell from 4 million tons to less than 1 million tons. Similar problems exist in other parts of the world. Overfishing and the demand for fish products as supplements in animal feed and fertilizer are all contributing to an ocean harvest that is unsustainable.

THE GREEN REVOLUTION

Between 1950 and 1980, the world experienced a dramatic increase in food output. The production of grain, the primary food source, almost tripled. Some of this growth was achieved by putting more acreage under cultivation, but the main reason was the so-called Green Revolution—the application of modern industrial technology to agriculture. This involved the mechanization of planting and harvesting, large-scale irrigation, extensive use of chemical fertilizers, pesticides, and herbicides, and the introduction of new, selectively bred strains of "high-yield" wheat, rice, and other crops. The whole package has been termed industrialized or energy-intensive agriculture, because both the equipment used and the manufacture of the necessary chemical ingredients depend on oil. Green Revolution techniques were first applied successfully in Mexico and the United States but were soon being pushed in the Third World as an essential part of aid programs.

In the 1950s, agricultural scientist Dr. Norman Borlaug developed a new strain of dwarf wheat that put more of its growth energy into the head of the grain and less energy into stalk growth. Not only was grain output increased, but the short stalks were sturdier and did not wither under heavy applications of nitrogen fertilizer, and they stood up better to mechanical harvesting. Breeding plants for maximum yield meant compromising other qualities, such as hardiness and resistance to pests and disease, so that the new variety of wheat required more pesticides and chemical protection. The end result was higher crop yields, but those yields could only be achieved by adopting a whole system of industrial inputs.

At first, the Green Revolution seemed like an agricultural miracle, producing millions of additional tons of wheat and rice throughout the world, but many environmentalists have since grown disillusioned. In the industrialized world, energy-intensive agriculture is proving to be unsustainable. It is dependent on nonrenewable fossil fuels. Chemical inputs are poisoning the soil and the water supply. Water itself is too scarce for the amount of irrigation required. Genetically engineered plants grow fast, but may not be hardy enough to survive plant blights or climate

Dr. Norman Borlaug, whose selectively bred, high-yield grains were the foundation of the Green Revolution. In 1970, Dr. Borlaug received the Nobel Prize for his efforts.

variations. Millions of farmers in the industrialized nations have been bankrupted, unable to keep up with the rising cost of petrochemicals and machinery. Intensive farming practices and efforts to maximize yields also degrade the land. The United States alone loses more than 3 billion tons of topsoil from its farm lands every year.

In the underdeveloped countries, in spite of some successes, the effects of the Green Revolution were pernicious. The new agricultural technology, with its emphasis on expensive machinery, was well suited to the United States, where it was developed and where there is much arable land and a comparatively small number of farmers. But in most Third World countries, where many farmers work a small amount of arable land, mechanization meant unemployment. Small farmers cannot possibly afford to mechanize or to buy expensive fertilizers and pesticides. The benefits of Green Revolution technology went principally to the large landowners and commercial crop producers. This increased divisions between rich and poor and encouraged cash crops for export at the expense of staple food production. It also produced environmental degradation on a large scale. As a result, world grain production has been leveling off since 1984, and per capita grain production has actually been falling—by 12% in Latin America since 1981, by 22% in Africa since 1967, and by 24% in India since 1983.

India's experience is typical. In the 1960s and early 1970s, using Dr. Borlaug's new wheat and its high-tech support system, India achieved record grain harvests and actually became self-sufficient in grain production. But in 1973 and 1974, when OPEC (Organization of Petroleum Exporting Countries) raised the price of oil, the cost to India of importing fertilizers increased by 600%. Only the largest and wealthiest farmers could afford to continue to practice this type of agriculture. By 1981, as its own reserves dwindled, India was buying grain from the United States in order to feed its people.

Though it undoubtedly helped to increase the world's food supply, the Green Revolution made underdeveloped nations more dependent on the industrialized nations for agricultural machinery, petrochemicals, and even for high-yield seed stock, whose patents were owned and controlled by the large corporations that could afford to invest in the biotechnology to develop them. To pay for these agricultural inputs, Third World nations went ever deeper into debt and pushed their farmers to produce more export crops to raise foreign exchange, thereby discouraging basic food production. It does not take a very large decrease in staple food production to create widespread hunger—this is not so much a matter of quantity as of price. A small drop in total quantity may raise the market price of food enough to prevent the poor from purchasing it, even if it is available.

Policies that favor large-scale commercial agriculture impoverish and bankrupt small farmers, who are often forced to sell their land to large farmers and move onto marginal lands. Land ownership becomes increasingly concentrated, and the overworking of the marginal lands degrades soil quality and renders it unproductive. Small farm income decreases, and more and more people lack the money to buy food staples and necessities. Recent history has shown that high-tech agriculture, though it may increase crop yields, also increases Third World poverty and hunger, and it enriches the industrialized world that provides the technology to a much greater extent than it promotes self-sufficiency in the underdeveloped world.

FOOD FOR EVERYONE?

Growing populations and shrinking rates of food production raise serious questions about the ability of the world to feed itself in the future. Population expert Anne H. Ehrlich of Stanford University is among those who are seriously worried about this issue: "The world population is now increasing by an average of 1.7 percent a year and is projected to expand from about 5 billion to over 10 billion before growth can be ended by humane means—that is, through limitation of births." This doubling of the human population is expected to occur by the second or third decade of the 21st century. Ehrlich resurrects the argument of the 19th-century English economist Thomas Malthus when she states that "rapid population growth quickly absorbs any gains made in economic development." Malthus has not been taken seriously for some time, because for more than a hundred years the world's industrialized societies have been able to sustain both economic expansion and population growth. Indeed, it seemed that population growth and the large, mobile labor force it created were necessary for expansion. But with the world reaching the limits of its finite resources, the Malthusian argument refuses to fade away.

Population pressures are particularly serious in the Third World. The countries of Africa, Latin America, and southern Asia have annual population growth rates exceeding 3% and even 4%, compared to less than 1% for the industrialized nations. Women in Africa on average bear six to eight children, compared to two children for women in the developed nations. At current rates, the East African nation of Kenya, to cite just one example, will double its population every 17 years. Because poor people often have large families out of economic necessity, family planning efforts in the Third World have not been very successful. According to Jodi L. Jacobson of the Worldwatch Institute, "Surveys confirm that half of the 463 million married women in developing countries outside China do not want more children." But high infant death rates create pressure for larger families, and poor parents need labor—whether it be another pair of hands to help in the fields or with housework—and someone to take care of them in old age in societies that provide no pensions, insurance, social welfare, or health care.

Such figures seem to indicate that overpopulation is as much a response to poverty as a cause of it. The history of the industrialized nations indicates that as living standards rise, birthrates go down without the need for intensive education in family planning. Large families provide a measure of economic security. When an affluent society provides that security through other means, people have fewer babies.

Many analysts are now questioning the whole concept of overpopulation as an explanation for Third World poverty. How many people is too many? Holland has a population density of over 1,100 people per square mile, but nobody is starving. Bolivia, on the other hand, has a density of only 12 people per square mile, and yet poverty and hunger are widespread. Before the revolution of 1949, China had only half as many people as it has today, and millions starved. Today, over 1 billion Chinese people are adequately fed. India, which has twice as much agricultural land as China and a lower population density, cannot feed its people. As for Mexico, Frances Moore Lappé and Rachel Schurman of the Institute for Food and Development Policy (also known as Food First) conclude that "despite a 37 percent decline in fertility rates since 1960, there is little evidence that the people are any less hungry."

Population expert Anne H. Ehrlich of Stanford University believes that if the world's population is not stabilized, its increasing size will dissipate all the gains of economic growth.

There does not appear to be any direct correlation between sheer numbers of people and hunger. Nor does there appear to be any connection between hunger and available food supplies. In a 1988 article in the journal *Social Policy*, Curtis Skinner noted that "the earth *presently* produces more than *twice* as much food as needed to provide all of its human inhabitants with a basic diet. If hundreds of millions of people are hungry today, it is not for lack of food, but because they are unable to pay for it." In their book *World Hunger: Twelve Myths*, Frances Moore Lappé and Joseph Collins note that in spite of recent declines in per capita grain production, "Rarely has the world seen such a glut of food looking for buyers. Increases in food production during the past 25 years have outstripped population growth by about 16 percent. Indeed, mountains of unsold grain on world markets have pushed prices downward over the past three decades." Many of the poorest nations of the world, though they may import basic grains to feed their people, are net exporters of agricultural products. G. Tyler Miller, Jr., in *Living in the Environment*, states that "Poverty—not lack of food production—is the chief cause of hunger, malnutrition, and premature death throughout the world."

Poverty is caused by lack of income, resulting from unemployment, underemployment, and, of particular relevance to the Third World, the pressures that make small farming unprofitable. Inequitable land distribution and concentration of wealth give large farmers enormous advantages. In hard times, small farmers cannot manage their debt, and they sell their land to the large farms. They then become tenants and wageworkers on other people's land. But the large farms, often producing for export, using advanced Western agricultural technology, need fewer laborers. Farm wages are kept low, and many people cannot find work at all. Development strategies and aid packages from the industrialized nations encourage this process of impoverishment by making farming even more expensive. In order to keep up with rising costs, both small and large farmers must work the land for all it can produce.

Over time, this increases soil erosion and environmental degradation. Green Revolution fertilizers and pesticides poison the soil and then run off into streams and rivers. Intensive irrigation waterlogs the soil, and when the water evaporates the salt content of the soil is increased, making it more difficult for plants to grow. The need for large amounts of irrigation water prompts many Third World governments to dam up rivers, creating more widespread environmental degradation. The need to maximize yields forces farmers to plant fields that they would normally leave fallow so that the soil would have time to regain nutrients. When this kind of overintensive agriculture is applied to marginal lands, it slowly turns them into desert.

The link between poverty and environmental degradation is so strong that when 160 nations met in Rio de Janeiro in June 1992 to devise a strategy for global environmental protection, the fifth principle of their draft agreement stated that "All states and all people shall cooperate in the essential task of eradicating poverty as an indispensable requirement for sustainable development, in order to decrease the disparities in standards of living and better meet the needs of the majority of the people of the world."

In most of the Third World, the root cause of poverty is land distribution—the way the land is divided up and used. In many tropical countries, land is wealth, and the statistics indicate that most rural inhabitants are land-poor. In Colombia, 66% of rural households own virtually no land; in Bangladesh, the number is 75%, and in Indonesia and Bolivia, 85% of rural households are landless.

Throughout the Third World, large tracts of land are either held unused, cultivated with export crops, or given over to cattle ranching to enrich a small class of the wealthy. In Africa today, about 13% of agricultural land is used to produce export crops—a portion of arable land removed from food production that is just large enough to affect supply so that the prices of food staples rise to a level that many poor Africans cannot afford. In Ecuador, prime agricultural land is used to grow bananas and roses for markets in North America while Indian peasants struggle to eke out a living on the hillsides of volcanoes in the Andes. As Susan George succinctly puts it in *How the Other Half Dies*, "The *structure* of landholdings has far more to do with erasing hunger than the amount of total population."

Development policies and aid packages from the industrialized nations that do not address—or that aggravate—these economic and social realities cannot solve the problem of world hunger or environmental degradation. The failure of the industrialized nations to recognize their own role in this process of impoverishment is likely to affect them in unexpected ways. For example, low prices on world markets for such commodities as coffee, corn, and cacao have driven many South American peasants to switch to a much more lucrative export—cocaine. In Colombia, Peru, and Bolivia, earnings from the sale of cocaine dwarf all other export earnings and in fact keep these debt-ridden economies afloat. In Bolivia, Susan George writes, "A hectare planted to coca can earn for its tenant at least US $1200 (£600 sterling) a year—sometimes much more. Compare this income to the average annual wage of a miner (US $827); or that of a factory worker ($649); or to the earnings of a non-coca-producing peasant ($150)."

What follows are case studies of how inappropriate development policies, along with many other factors, have contributed to the creation of famine and environmental degradation in specific regions of the world.

SUB-SAHARAN AFRICA

The African Sahel, so often the focus of attention because of the famines that afflict millions there, is a large geographical region in West Africa that lies just to the south of the north African coastal states and the Sahara desert. Sahel comes from the Arabic word for shore, because the inhabitants regarded the bordering Sahara as an uninhabitable sea. Today, the Sahel embraces the countries of Mauritania, Senegal, Gambia, Mali, Upper Volta, Niger, and Chad. Though they are not in West Africa, the Sudan, Ethiopia, and Somalia are often grouped with Sahelian countries because they have experienced similar problems.

Though often described as semiarid, the Sahel contains a variety of ecosystems, ranging from desert in the north to savannas, grasslands, and even tropical rainforests in the south. Nevertheless, for a large part of the Sahel, rainfall averages from only one-sixth to one-half of what cities such as New York or Chicago experience. The people of the area survive in a narrow band between the northern desert and the tsetse fly belt to the south, where neither human beings nor cattle are safe from trypanosomiasis, the "sleeping sickness" that makes its victims lethargic and finally comatose. Peculiarities of climate mean that every five or ten years even these meager rains may fail. In recent decades, periodic famine and starvation in the Sahel have forced millions of Africans to abandon their homes and march off to refugee camps to receive food aid from the western nations—a pitiable spectacle that has been well documented by the world's media.

The Sahel, however, was not always like this. From about A.D. 500 to 1500, there were great kingdoms throughout this region of Africa. In spite of the climate, the area was for the most part prosperous and stable. Extensive trade in gold, copper, iron, salt, and slaves was conducted across the desert caravan routes to

The famine-stricken countries of Sub Saharan Africa, where insufficient rainfall, the intensive cultivation of export crops, the overgrazing of land by livestock, high rates of population growth, and civil war have all combined to destroy what was once a self-sufficient economy.

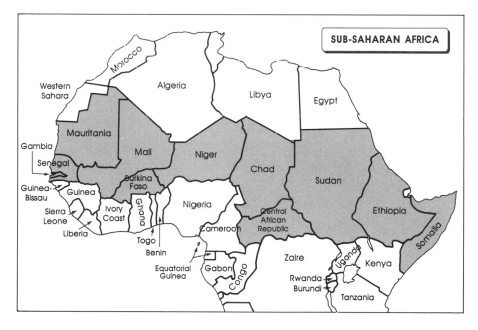

the states of North Africa, and the royalty of the kingdoms of Ghana, Mali, and Songhay lived in luxury. More important, the ordinary people of the region had learned to produce an abundance of food through a complex system of adaptation to available resources.

Life was sustained through the activities of small farmers and pastoralists, or animal herders, who grazed their herds where nothing but grasses would grow. Animal herding is a nomadic activity. As the grasses of one region are eaten, herders must move their animals on to another region. The Fulani tribesmen who kept cattle, sheep, goats, donkeys, and camels developed a close relationship with the local farmers as they moved through various areas, allowing their herds to manure the farmers' fields and trading meat, hides, and milk for millet, sorghum, rice, beans, and corn. Elaborate social customs controlled the relationships between farmers and pastoralists and determined land usage and water rights. This system was not perfect, and there were periods of famine, but for a thousand years the people of the region prospered and produced a sufficient agricultural surplus to provide a modest measure of protection against hard times.

That situation began to change when France became interested in West Africa. The French first penetrated the region in the middle of the 17th century and established complete control by 1900. The effects of this colonial enterprise were devastating. The war of conquest itself destroyed many farms and disrupted the caravan routes. The construction of port cities along the Gulf of Guinea, along with the laying of railroads, destroyed trade with North Africa and bankrupted many merchants. Local crafts were ruined by cheap French-manufactured imports. Many young West Africans were drafted to fight in the French army in Europe.

The most destructive change, however, came in the 18th century, when the French colonial administration began to impose taxes on the West Africans. Farmers who practice subsistence agriculture—who eat what they grow or barter portions of it for other necessities—are not part of a cash economy and cannot earn money to pay taxes. As it became necessary to grow crops that the French would pay for in cash, the area given over to the cultivation of food staples—millet and sorghum—gradually diminished as an ever-growing amount of land was planted with coffee, sugarcane, and peanuts. All of these were crops the French were eager to import to their homeland.

As this new agricultural system replaced the precolonial one, less food was available to the populace, whose traditional "cushion" against hard times was lost. Malnutrition and famine became commonplace as commercial agriculture disrupted the relationships between farmers and animal herders. As more land was cleared and enclosed to meet the growing demand of the French for these new crops, forests were cut down, and even marginal lands were put under cultivation. These marginal lands, of course, were where the pastoralists grazed their herds, and they were driven onto even poorer land. The animals suffered and died, and there was no surplus to trade for the food that was no longer available in any case.

In the 1960s, France began to relinquish political control of the countries of West Africa, but these nations remained economically dependent on export crops and the foreign customers who bought them. Peanut production throughout the region increased as farmers applied new seed varieties, fertilizers, new mechanical implements, and planted the land they would normally have left fallow. This kind of overintensive farming played havoc with the environment. According to Lappé and Collins, "growing the same crops year after year on the same land, without any mixing of crops, trees, and livestock, rapidly ruined the soils. Just two successive years of peanuts can rob the soil in Senegal of almost a third of its organic matter." Overproduction contributed to a glut on the world market, a situation that was aggravated by the growth of the soybean industry in the United States. Soybean oil proved a good, cheap substitute for peanut oil, and on European markets the price of peanuts fell by more than 20%. With the costs of farming increasing and the price of crops falling, many farmers went into debt—the first step toward loss of land and impoverishment.

The pastoralists, pushed onto marginal lands, suffered a similar fate. In the 1950s and 1960s, France had tried to encourage West African meat exports in order to satisfy the European demand for beef. By introducing a number of improve-

The lands of the Sahel are overfarmed, overgrazed, and slowly turning into desert. Desperate for food, this goat climbed a tree to get at its leaves and died in the branches.

ments—well digging, antibiotic inoculations, refrigerated storage and shipping facilities—European technocrats were able to help Fulani tribesmen vastly increase the size of their herds, but nobody could create new pasturelands for these animals when the best land was reserved for commercial crops. The larger herds overgrazed and destroyed the marginal lands, turning them into more desert; then the herds—the Fulani's only source of income—starved and died. By the early 1970s, the Sahel was in the midst of a widespread famine that has become a semipermanent feature of life in the region up to the present day.

CENTRAL AMERICA

The countries of Central America—Mexico, Guatemala, El Salvador, Honduras, Nicaragua, Costa Rica, and Panama—offer another interesting example of the consequences of the unequal relationship between the Third World and the industialized nations. These nations of Central America, which all have tropical climates and plenty of sun and rain, are productive agricultural areas, but at least 50% of the inhabitants of the region do not receive an adequate diet, and the numbers of the hungry are increasing. As a result, these countries are among the most politically unstable and violence-prone states in the world.

Since the 1800s, settlers have been slowly transforming the lands of Central America to produce crops for export, a trend that accelerated greatly after 1950, when the United States became the dominant political and economic power in the region. Small farms and Indian communal lands were acquired and merged into big estates—haciendas and latifundios—to facilitate the mass production of coffee, bananas, cotton, sugarcane, and beef. As small farmers failed and became landless laborers in the barrios and slums of the cities, the acreage devoted to basic foods such as corn and beans decreased. In 1987, Central America had to *import* three-quarters of a million tons of food to sustain its people. Yet it seems absurd to point to underdevelopment or overpopulation as the source of the problem when the same region in the same year *exported* over 4.5 million tons of cash crops.

The problem of hunger in Central America is caused by inequalities in the distribution of land and in its use. While the industrialized nations benefit from the northward flow of cheap agricultural products, the result for the majority of Central Americans is impoverishment and hunger. Commercial plantation-style agriculture reduces production of staple foods and impoverishes farmers, who are thrown onto marginal lands. Exports rise, but the majority of Central Americans are left unable to earn the income to buy what food is available. In El Salvador, for example, according to Tom Barry in *Roots of Rebellion*, 60% of all coffee production takes place on just 4% of the farms, which are owned by 36 families. About 95% of El Salvador's farms are considered too small to support even a single family. Similar situations exist throughout Central America in the production of cotton, sugarcane, and beef.

THE FUTURE

Economic development has come to an almost complete halt in many of the poor nations, and poverty and hunger are on the rise, both relative to living standards in the rich nations and in absolute numbers of people affected. World population continues to grow unchecked and is beginning to exceed the "carrying capacity" of the environment. Though the rich nations of the world have successfully converted parts of the underdeveloped world into plantations for the production of cheap agricultural products, failure to effect genuine economic reform in the poorer nations will—perhaps in the very near future—prove to have been tragically shortsighted.

The solutions to these problems, like the problems themselves, are invariably complex, but at the very least they will require a commitment to genuine land reform and a reversal of the trend toward large-scale commercial agriculture in poor countries. The production of staple foods needs to be be encouraged, even at the expense of export crops, and the industrialized nations must be willing to extend debt relief to the poorer countries as they make their way to economic self-sufficiency. Natural fertilizers and natural methods of pest control need to be promoted in order to prevent environmental degradation and reduce the cost of farming. Most of all, nations must begin to look at agriculture first as a means of feeding and employing people, not as a means of solving trade deficits.

Alan B. Durning of the Worldwatch Institute summarizes the problem quite dramatically: "Failure to launch an all-out assault on poverty will not only stain the history of our age, it will guarantee the destruction of much of our shared biosphere. For although environmental damage penalizes the poor more consistently and severely than it does the wealthy, the circle eventually becomes complete. . . . The fate of the fortunate is immutably bonded to the fate of the dispossessed through the land, water, and air; in an ecologically endangered world, poverty is a luxury we can no longer afford."

A sustainable society will have to recycle and reuse as many products as it possibly can. Here shredded telephone books are bundled up for shipment to mills that will turn them into new paper.

chapter 5

THE SUSTAINABLE
ECONOMY

"Most people," state Paul and Anne Ehrlich in *The Population Explosion*, "do not recognize that, at least in rich nations,
economic growth is the disease, not the cure." Advocates of a
steady-state economy argue that, in today's world, high rates of
economic growth translate into the squandering of limited natural
resources, the generation of hazardous wastes, an obscenely
luxurious life-style for some and starvation for others, overall
economic insecurity, and myriad social problems.

Not everyone agrees. In *The Resourceful Earth*,
economists Julian L. Simon and Herman Kahn point to the
long-term achievements of industrial society—increased life
expectancy, a declining birthrate, and increased food
output—and dismiss environmental degradation as minimal and
exaggerated. With regard to economic growth, Simon and Kahn
"are confident that the nature of the physical world permits
continued improvement in humankind's economic lot in the long
run, indefinitely." Their confidence is based largely on their belief
in society's ability to devise creative solutions for each new
problem created by the march of civilization. By contrast, many

environmentalists view each new solution as a cause of new problems.

Whether the future proves the optimists or the pessimists to be correct, some global economic and environmental problems are serious enough to require immediate action. The future discovery of some new energy technology matters little to the 1 billion poor people inhabiting the earth, whose economic supports are collapsing now. If for no other reason, the industrialized countries need to rethink their philosophy of unlimited growth and consider the alternatives.

How would a steady-state economy actually work? Herman Daly of the World Bank, in his book *Steady-State Economics*, advocates a kind of managed capitalism, with free markets functioning within certain limits, or what he calls "institutional preconditions." One such precondition would limit the growth of population by adopting a proposal put forward by Kenneth Boulding for transferable birth licenses. Individuals would be required to obtain such licenses in order to have children. The state would decide how many new people the economy could absorb and equitably distribute birth licenses for that

Herman E. Daly, senior environmental economist at the World Bank, was one of the first economists to put forward a blueprint for a sustainable society.

number. Once distributed, the licenses could be freely bought and sold by people who did or did not want more children. Only the total number of births would be controlled, with minimum interference in the private lives of families, unlike the current one-child policy in the People's Republic of China. One objection to this idea, however, is that a free market for babies, like all free markets, tends to "marginalize," or drive out of the market, the poor, who cannot afford the licenses.

Daly hopes to overcome this problem through another of his preconditions—maximum and minimum limits on personal income. A minimum personal income would lift many people out of poverty and enable them to become participants in economic life. A maximum personal income would limit social inequalities in the distribution of goods and services and curb the acquisitive instinct that lies behind unrestrained economic growth. Daly suggests that the upper income limit might be $100,000 or $200,000: "A range of inequality would continue to exist to reward real differences in effort, risk, and conditions of work." The third element in Daly's plan is the creation of depletion quotas for natural resources. The state would determine how much of its natural resources should be used up at any one time and auction off to producers the right to buy these resources. Having purchased only the right to buy a fixed quantity of raw materials, the producers must still compete in the marketplace and pay resource suppliers market prices for raw materials. By controlling the quantity of resources used rather than their price, the state can establish a rate of resource use that is sustainable. At the opposite end of the production process there is an absolute, foreseeable limit on the amount of waste and pollution that a fixed quantity of materials can generate. Daly also believes that limits on available resources will promote their conservation and efficient use. A fixed supply, however, traded on a free market, will lead to higher prices for these resources. "Higher prices on basic resources are absolutely necessary," counters Daly. "Any plan that refuses to face up to this necessity is worthless."

The whole idea behind Daly's blueprint is to achieve "limits on the population of human bodies; and limits on the population of artifacts" as well as "limits on the degree of in-equality in the distribution of artifacts." The goal is to establish a sustainable rate of "throughput," the rate at which material resources are put through the production process and transformed into commodities. What must be changed, Daly says, is the commitment to "terminal hyper-growthmania."

Economists of various political persuasions are wary of the idea of a steady-state free market economy. Mainstream economic analysis holds that a free market economy cannot stand still, and that continued growth in output is necessary to maintain high levels of employment and to avoid economic slump. Paul A. Samuelson and William D. Nordhaus, in the 13th edition of the popular textbook *Economics*, state that "a prosperous period may come to an end, not simply because sales have gone down, but merely because production and sales have stabilized at a high level." Left-wing critic Michael Parenti paints a more desperate picture: "To stand still amidst the growth of competitors is to decline, not only relatively but absolutely, causing a firm's financial structure to collapse. The dynamics of a modern market economy—the accumulation of profit and the need to invest surplus capital, the demand for strategic overseas materials and new markets, the fluctuations in consumer spending, the in-stabilities of old markets, the threat of recession and depression, the pressures of domestic and foreign competition—all these things force corporations into a restless, endless drive to expand. Those ecologists who dream of a 'no-growth capitalism,' better to preserve the environment, do not seem to realize that the concept is an oxymoron."

Whatever one's position, it is clear that management of a steady-state free market economy involves state intervention on an unprecedented level. But many environmentalists argue that because of the unwillingness of firms to pay external costs, unmanaged capitalism cannot succeed in coping with

These two diagrams, supplied by the group Zero Population Growth, embody the environmentalist's argument that economic activity is not a perpetual motion machine, but draws on the finite resources of the surrounding environment.

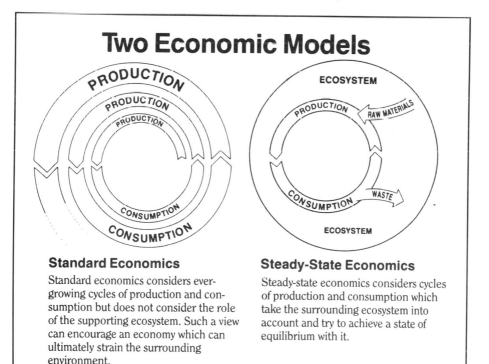

Two Economic Models

Standard Economics

Standard economics considers ever-growing cycles of production and consumption but does not consider the role of the supporting ecosystem. Such a view can encourage an economy which can ultimately strain the surrounding environment.

Steady-State Economics

Steady-state economics considers cycles of production and consumption which take the surrounding ecosystem into account and try to achieve a state of equilibrium with it.

environmental problems. They argue that, with a sustainable economy, at least there will be resources left to be put to use by those who come afterward, who may have some better ideas about how to manage their world.

Whatever large-scale controlling institutions are created, the micromanagement of any sustainable society will change the way people live and work and force them to make difficult choices. Achieving sustainable rates of energy consumption will be the biggest hurdle, and it is not at all clear that new technologies can solve this problem. Nevertheless, economic incentives will have to be created to promote the development of every renewable energy resource.

Hydroelectric power takes energy out of flowing water, which is caused to flow by a combination of solar and gravitational energy. It is therefore renewable, but the ecological impact of dams is often catastrophic in terms of forest and wildlife destruction and water diversion. The answer may lie in leaving the world's bigger rivers alone and employing smaller turbine systems designed to provide electricity locally. China has over 85,000 small hydroelectric units operating now.

Solar energy, collected in the form of heat by parabolic mirrors or converted directly into electricity by photovoltaic cells, is perhaps the most environmentally benign energy source. But the amount of solar energy striking a given surface area is very small. The technology presently requires large areas of land covered with many collecting devices in order to generate only a relatively small amount of electricity. In its present state of development, solar energy holds many benefits for individual households and local communities, but it is unlikely to supply the large amounts of energy required by industry. Power companies may resist its expanded use because the collection of solar energy cannot be centralized and controlled in the same way as conventional power generation. Anyone with a few pieces of polished aluminum can fry an egg on a sunny day in his or her backyard, without the need for a central generating station or a power grid operated by a utility company.

Biomass energy—the burning of unused organic materials such as crop residues, animal dung, and garbage, or the growing of crops to be made into alternative fuels—is already in use in some countries. In Brazil, half of all the automobile fuel used consists of alcohol fermented from sugarcane. But in a world where both natural fertilizers and land for growing food are in short supply, using biomass to create fuel for machinery may take scarce land away from food production or starve soils of replenishing organic matter.

Wind power has been used for centuries, and in both Denmark and the state of California "wind farms" have been generating electricity for over 15 years. But only certain geographical regions can exploit this source of energy, and only when the wind blows. *Geothermal energy* involves the extraction of heat from water that has been in contact with hot layers of rock deep below the earth's surface. Here, too, only certain areas of the world have the right geology to make this process workable. *Ocean energy*—extracting energy from the force of moving waves and tides—has been sucessfully tried in France and Norway.

If oil and coal can be thought of as forms of stored or concentrated energy, then solar, wind, geothermal, and ocean

This array of photovoltaic cells, which converts sunlight directly into electricity, uses up no terrestrial natural resources and generates no pollution—an ideal energy source for a steady-state economy.

sources can be thought of as "real-time" energy. A sustainable society will need to increase its dependence on these real-time energy sources, but they simply do not exist in concentrated forms. It will cost more, and take longer, to accumulate energy from these new sources. The cost may not be an obstacle if petroleum becomes scarce and its price begins to rise, but the slower rate of accumulation imposes definite limits on industrial growth. These new energy technologies require matching energy conservation policies.

Conservation will involve the recycling of materials such as paper, steel, glass, aluminum, and other substances, thereby reducing the amount of energy used to make new materials. Since saving and reusing these materials reduces costs, industries have built-in incentives to practice energy efficiency, and many corporations have already achieved a great deal in this area. The efforts of industry must be matched elsewhere—in more efficient home heating, more efficient appliances, and most of all, in the design of more fuel-efficient automobiles. Some groups regard the automobile as so crucial to solving the environmental crisis that they advocate a large increase in the tax on gasoline to cure Americans of their addiction to cheap energy. In Europe and Japan, a gallon of gasoline costs two and a half to three times what it costs American motorists. "The current U.S. gasoline tax does not begin to cover all the costs associated with cars and trucks," states the Global Tomorrow Coalition. "Expenses such as road building and maintenance, lost tax revenues from paved-over land, traffic regulation, accidents and health care, and driver education may require up to $300 billion a year in subsidies by local, state, and federal governments."

Are there no easier answers to the energy question lying just beyond the horizon? Is it not possible that technological innovation will rescue an oil-starved world before it is too late? No one can say that it is not possible. There may yet be a safe way to employ nuclear power. Or scientists may move beyond the *fission* reactor to the *fusion* reactor, producing plentiful energy with relatively little radioactive waste from the elements in seawater. The new field of superconductivity may make electrical generation and transmission vastly more efficient.

Not all the secrets of the universe are known. But certain fundamental secrets—such as the laws of thermodynamics—are known only too well. These laws state in unequivocal terms that whatever technology the world chooses, it will not get something for nothing. In the process of transforming the shape and composition of materials, industrial society will degrade the available energy supply in an irreversible way. The issue of energy management will always be with us.

AGRICULTURE

In spite of large gains in output, global agricultural production has become too dependent on expensive chemical inputs derived from nonrenewable fuels. Like the industrial use of energy, this kind of agriculture is not sustainable. It degrades topsoils and tends to benefit not farmers so much as the banks, corporations, and industries that supply credit, fertilizer, pesticides, machinery, and seed. Small farmers, even in the industrialized countries, go bankrupt by the millions as agribusinesses reorganize the land into commercial farming enterprises large enough to make this new industrial agriculture cost efficient.

There is no shortage of technical fixes for an alternative, sustainable type of agriculture. The use of pesticides can be reduced through integrated pest management, a program that relies on natural insect predators, selective breeding of pest-resistant plant species, and *intercropping* —the mixing of different plant species in the same plot. Intercropping also improves soil fertility. Natural fertilizers can replace artificial ones, and increased crop rotation will give soils a chance to recover their vitality. There are many techniques for making irrigation more efficient, and raising the price of water to farmers would encourage them to use these techniques.

Purely technical fixes, however, cannot provide the whole solution. Energy-intensive agriculture arose out of the same competitive, expansionist drive to increase production that motivates all business growth and innovation. It is an integral part of modern capitalism, and it has transformed society. Modern agriculture is much more than a few chemicals applied to crops. It involves banking and credit institutions, research stations and gene banks, commodities markets, manufacturers of farm machinery, storage and transportation facilities, food processing and packaging plants, and supermarket chains. Most of the money people pay for agricultural products goes not to the primary grower but to the businesses that turn potatoes into potato chips and oats into breakfast cereal.

The introduction of sustainable agriculture requires changing an extremely complex system of food production. That system evolved as part of the normal competitive drive of various enterprises to cut their costs, as every business strives to do, by increasing the amount of capital and technology and reducing the amount of labor that goes into their products. This has led to the *agribusiness*—an agricultural enterprise owned by a large corporation that also owns and controls storage, transportation, processing, and packaging businesses. More independent, decentralized, and labor-intensive farming threatens this whole system, and change may be resisted. Moreover, sustainable agriculture must prove itself to be profitable. "Low input" farming techniques—those that do not require large inputs of fertilizer, pesticide, machinery, or water—do tend to reduce the size of harvests, at least in comparison with conventional farming practices in the industrialized nations. Some results of the Low Input-Sustainable Agriculture (LISA) program of the U.S. Department of Agriculture seem to suggest that this kind of farming can be economically competitive.

In the underdeveloped world, technology alone is not the answer to agricultural difficulties. Technology has in fact often made conditions worse, because only the rich can afford it. The root of the problem is economic and political, and the issues that must be directly confronted are land reform and debt relief. Third World governments with large numbers of rural poor must ask themselves if agriculture is just to be a means of maximizing capital return, like any other business, or a means of feeding people. If it is to be a means of feeding people, then more of them must become productively involved in agriculture, not just so that more food is produced but so that more people are provided with a source of income to buy it. This means taking land away from those who have a lot and giving it to those who have none—an explosive proposal that challenges powerful economic and political forces and that has rarely occurred without violent revolution.

Redistribution of land and rural development programs will slow economic growth, but more people will share in its benefits. These programs will, however, be challenged by large landowners, urban elites, development "experts," foreign banks, and transnational corporations that own and control the plantations and processing plants, as well as foreign governments opposed to breaking up the old dependencies. Something beyond self-interest will be required of all parties if these issues are to be resolved without violent conflict.

Since massive Third World foreign debt promotes commercial agriculture at the expense of food production and encourages environmental degradation, some form of debt relief is essential for these nations. But how can Western banks write off $1 trillion in unrecoverable losses, especially in a period characterized by bad loans, bank failures, and low rates of savings? There is no easy answer, but industrialized countries need to come up with one before austerity measures make Third World nations politically unstable, or they simply choose to default on their loans without asking, which will have enormous repercussions for the banks and all other businesses that have to borrow from them.

THE NEW WORLD ORDER

The issue of free trade and of a single, integrated world economic order is also difficult to resolve. Mainstream economists can demonstrate mathematically that free trade is good for businesses and consumers in all countries. Businesses have access to larger markets, and consumers are presented with a wider variety of goods at competitive prices. But consumers are also workers, and wherever investment capital and enterprises themselves are free to move around the world in search of ideal business conditions and the lowest costs, there will be a downward pressure on wages to the levels paid in the poorest countries. Many workers experienced this problem of low-wage competition when the European Economic Community, the Common Market, was formed in 1957 and member nations began to eliminate tariffs and quotas between their borders. In the 1990s, many Americans continue to watch jobs disappear as entrepreneurs shift their operations to low-wage countries such as Mexico. Free trade is clearly a double-edged sword.

And mathematical models aside, when disadvantaged countries begin to engage in international trade, they find many conditions stacked against them. They must sell cheap raw materials to buy expensive manufactured imports, and they must go into debt to keep doing so. They are burdened with high prices for energy supplies and new technology. Foreign investors demand cheap labor, low taxes, and minimal environmental regulation. Industrialized nations fear their growth as competitors. The more poor nations integrate themselves into the global economy, the poorer they get. International free markets, like all unregulated free markets, evolve in such a way as to make some participants very rich and others very poor.

There are many "ifs" regarding the effort to eliminate global problems of poverty, hunger, and environmental degradation. If the rich nations adopt some kind of steady-state model and restrict the purely quantitative growth of their economies, if they grant the poor nations debt relief, if they develop an "affirmative action" strategy that grants to poor nations advantages in international trade and in access to energy and technology, if they recognize the need of poor nations to be more self-sufficient and less integrated into an unfairly structured global economy—at least until they can function as equal partners—there is a fair chance that these problems might be brought under control. But those are a lot of very big "ifs," and they require new thinking about the purpose of economic activity in human society.

APPENDIX: FOR MORE INFORMATION

Agency for International
  Development
State Building
320 21st Street NW
Washington, DC 20523
(202) 647-1850

American Council for an
  Energy-Efficient Economy
1001 Connecticut Avenue NW
Washington, DC 20036
(202) 429-8873

Agri-Energy Roundtable
Suite 300
2550 M Street NW
Washington, DC 20037
(202) 887-0528

Appropriate Technology
  International
1331 H Street NW
Washington, DC 20005
(202) 879-2900

The Brookings Institute
1775 Massachusetts Avenue NW
Washington, DC 20036
(202) 797-6105

Center of Concern
3700 13th Street NE

Washington, DC 20017
(202) 635-2757

Council on Foreign Relations
58 East 68th Street
New York, NY 10021
(212) 734-0400

Environmental Project on
  Central America
Earth Island International
  Center
13 Columbus Avenue
San Francisco, CA 94111

Food and Agriculture
  Organization of the United
  Nations
1001 22nd Street NW
Washington, DC 20437
(202) 653-2398

Global Tomorrow Coalition
1325 G Street NW
Washington, DC 20005
(202) 628-4016

The Hunger Project
1 Madison Avenue
Suite 8A
New York, NY 10010
(212) 532-4255

Institute for Alternative
  Agriculture
9200 Edmonston Road
Greenbelt, MD 20770
(301) 441-9777

Institute for Food and
  Development Policy (Food
  First)
145 9th Street
San Francisco, CA 94103
(415) 864-8555

Inter-Hemispheric Education
  Resource Center
Box 4506
Albuquerque, NM 87196
(505) 842-8288

International Food Policy
  Research Institute
1776 Massachusetts Avenue NW
Washington, DC 20036
(202) 862-5600

International Monetary Fund
700 19th Street NW
Washington, DC 20431
(202) 623-7000

Maryknoll Mission Center of
  New England
50 Dunster Road
Chestnut Hill, MA 02167
(617) 232-8050

National Clearinghouse on
  Development Education
c/o American Forum for
  Education in a Global Age
45 John Street
Suite 1200
New York, NY 10038
(212) 732-8606

Natural Resources Defense
  Council
1350 New York Avenue NW
Washington, DC 20005
(202) 783-7800

Oxfam America
115 Broadway
Boston, MA 02116
(617) 482-1211

Population Council
1 Dag Hammarskjold Plaza
New York, NY 10017
(212) 644-1300

Population Crisis Committee
1120 19th Street NW
Washington, DC 20036
(202) 659-1833

Third World Women's Project
c/o Institute for Policy Studies
1601 Connecticut Avenue NW
Washington, DC 20009
(202) 234-9382, ext. 234

Union of Concerned Scientists
26 Church Street
Cambridge, MA 02238
(617) 547-5552

United Nations Environment
  Program
1889 F Street NW
Washington, DC 20006
(202) 289-8456

U.S. Department of Energy
Conservation and Renewable
  Energy Division
1000 Independence Avenue SW
Washington, DC 20585
(202) 586 9220

World Bank
1818 H Street NW
Washington, DC 20433
(202) 477-1234

Worldwatch Institute
1776 Massachusetts Avenue
  NW
Washington, DC 20036
(202) 452-1999

Zero Population Growth
1400 16th Street NW
Suite 320
Washington, DC 20036
(202) 332-2200

FURTHER READING

Ascher, William, and Robert Healy. *Natural Resource Policymaking in Developing Countries.* Durham: Duke University Press, 1990.

Barry, Tom. *Roots of Rebellion.* Boston: South End Press, 1987.

Branford, Sue, and Benardo Kucinski. *The Debt Squads.* London: Zed Books, 1988.

Brown, Lester R. *Building a Sustainable Society.* New York: Norton, 1981.

Cowell, Adrian. *The Decade of Destruction.* New York: Henry Holt and Company, 1991.

Daly, Herman E. *Steady-State Economics.* Washington, DC: Island Press, 1991.

Delamaide, Darrell. *Debt Shock.* New York: Anchor Books, 1985.

Doyle, Jack. *Altered Harvest.* New York: Penguin Books, 1985.

Ehrlich, Paul R., and Anne H. Ehrlich. *The Population Explosion.* New York: Simon & Schuster, 1990.

Foley, Gerald. *The Energy Question.* London: Penguin Books, 1987.

Fowler, Cary, and Pat Mooney. *Shattering.* Tucson: University of Arizona Press, 1990.

Franke, Richard W., and Barbara H. Chasin. *Seeds of Famine.* Totowa, NJ: Allanheld, Osmun & Co., 1980.

George, Susan. *The Debt Boomerang*. Boulder, CO: Westview Press, 1992.

———. *A Fate Worse Than Debt*. New York: Grove Weidenfeld, 1990.

———. *How the Other Half Dies*. Totowa, NJ: Rowman & Allanheld, 1983.

———. *Ill Fares the Land*. London: Penguin Books, 1990.

George, Susan, and Nigel Paige. *Food for Beginners*. London: Writers and Readers Publishing Cooperative Society, 1982.

Global Tomorrow Coalition. *The Global Ecology Handbook*. Boston: Beacon Press, 1990.

Hecht, Susanna, and Alexander Cockburn. *The Fate of the Forest*. New York: HarperCollins, 1990.

Heilbroner, Robert L., and Lester C. Thurow. *Economics Explained*. New York: Simon & Schuster, 1987.

Hollist, W. Ladd, and F. LaMond Tullis. *Pursuing Food Security*. Boulder, CO: Lynne Rienner Publishers, 1987.

Kennedy, Paul. *The Rise and Fall of the Great Powers*. New York: Random House, 1987.

Lappé, Frances More, and Joseph Collins. *World Hunger: Twelve Myths*. New York: Grove Press, 1986.

Lean, Geoffrey, Don Hinrichsen, and Adam Markham. *World Wildlife Fund Atlas of the Environment*. New York: Prentice Hall, 1990.

Lee, Susan. *ABZs of Economics*. New York: Pocket Books, 1987.

Lewis, W. Arthur. *The Theory of Economic Growth*. Homewood, IL: Irwin, 1955.

McConnell, Campbell R., and Stanley L. Brue. *Economics.* 11th Edition. New York: McGraw-Hill, 1990.

Miller, G. Tyler, Jr. *Living in the Environment.* 6th Edition. Belmont, CA: Wadsworth, 1990.

Mittelman, James H. *Out from Underdevelopment.* New York: St. Martin's, 1988.

Myers, Dr. Norman. *Gaia: An Atlas of Planet Management.* London: Gaia Books, 1984.

Palmer, R. R. *A History of the Modern World.* 2nd Edition. New York: Knopf, 1961.

Pincus, John A. *Reshaping the World Economy.* Englewood Cliffs, NJ: Prentice Hall, 1968.

Polesetsky, Matthew. *Global Resources: Opposing Viewpoints.* San Diego: Greenhaven Press, 1991.

Roddick, Jackie. *The Dance of the Millions.* London: Latin American Bureau, 1988.

Rohr, Janelle. *The Third World: Opposing Viewpoints.* San Diego: Greenhaven Press, 1989.

Samuelson, Paul A., and William D. Nordhaus. *Economics.* 14th Edition. New York: McGraw-Hill, 1992.

Schumacher, E. F. *Small Is Beautiful.* New York: HarperCollins, 1989.

Simon, Julian L., and Herman Kahn. *The Resourceful Earth.* Oxford: Basil Blackwell, 1984.

Solkoff, Joel. *The Politics of Food.* San Francisco: Sierra Club Books, 1985.

Thomson, Robert. *Green Gold*. London: Latin American Bureau, 1987.

Ward, Barbara. *Progress for a Small Planet*. New York: Norton, 1979.

World Commission on Environment and Development. *Our Common Future*. Oxford: Oxford University Press, 1987.

Worldwatch Institute. *State of the World 1990*. New York: Norton, 1990.

Yergin, Daniel, and Martin Hillenbrand. *Global Insecurity*. Boston: Houghton Mifflin, 1982.

GLOSSARY

acid rain Precipitation containing sulfuric and nitric acids formed from the burning of fossil fuels; also called acid deposition.

agribusiness An agricultural enterprise combining the production, processing, storage, and distribution of farm goods, sometimes including the manufacture and distribution of farm equipment and supplies.

capital goods Nonconsumer products (such as factories, furnaces, tools, and machinery) used to produce and distribute consumer products.

cash crops Crops produced for their market value, such as coffee, cotton, and tobacco, which are not consumed locally by the people who grow them.

default Failure to fulfill a contract, agreement, or duty.

deforestation The destruction of any forest by human beings—most often used in reference to the current situation in the tropics, where rainforests are being leveled by millions of acres yearly. The planting of forests to offset this trend is called reforestation.

depreciation The lowering of a value.

erosion Process by which soil is carried away from a region by water or wind; can occur naturally or because of human activities, including deforestation, overgrazing, and various farming methods.

external costs The social and environmental costs of producing and using a product that are not included in the market price of that product.

fission The splitting of an atomic nucleus, resulting in the release of large amounts of energy.

free market A market in which governments do not interfere with the exchange of goods; supply and demand determine price and quantity produced.

fusion The union of atomic nuclei, resulting in the release of enormous quantities of energy.

global warming The warming of the earth's atmosphere due to the trapping of infrared radiation by gases such as carbon dioxide and methane; also known as the greenhouse effect.

gross national product (GNP) Total market value in current dollars of all finished goods and services produced by an economy during a year.

inflation An economic condition in which prices rise.

intercropping Growing two or more crops on the same plot at the same time.

natural resources Industrial materials and capacities, such as mineral deposits and waterpower, which are supplied by nature.

neocolonialism The economic and political policies by which a great power indirectly maintains or extends its influence over other areas or people.

net value The value remaining after total liabilities are subtracted from total assets.

per capita income Income per person.

steady-state economy   An economy that would regulate growth so as not to deplete the limited resources of the earth.

trade deficit   A debt incurred by a country which imports more that it exports.

true costs   The sum of the internal cost (the direct cost of producing a product) and the external cost (the social and environmental costs not included in the price of the product).

INDEX

P I C T U R E   C R E D I T S

AP/Wide World Photos: pp. 12, 34, 38, 46, 68, 71, 74, 86, 90; Courtesy
Herman E. Daly: p. 92; Department of Energy: pp. 25, 98; Photo by Dennis
Johns: p. 78; Library of Congress: p. 59; Courtesy Rainforest Action Network:
p. 56; ©Rick Reinhard 1984: p. 31; Courtesy Julian L. Simon: p. 44; Gary
Tong: p. 73; USDA Photo: p. 29; World Development Report 1988: p. 61;
Shirley Zeiberg: p. 18; Zero Population Growth: p. 95

Conversion Table

(From U.S./English system units to metric system units)

Length

1 inch = 2.54 centimeters
1 foot = 0.305 meters
1 yard = 0.91 meters
1 statute mile = 1.6 kilometers (km.)

Area

1 square yard = 0.84 square meters
1 acre = 0.405 hectares
1 square mile = 2.59 square km.

Liquid Measure

1 fluid ounce = 0.03 liters
1 pint (U.S.) = 0.47 liters
1 quart (U.S.) = 0.95 liters
1 gallon (U.S.) = 3.78 liters

Weight and Mass

1 ounce = 28.35 grams
1 pound = 0.45 kilograms
1 ton = 0.91 metric tons

Temperature

1 degree Fahrenheit = 0.56 degrees Celsius or centigrade, but to convert from actual Fahrenheit scale measurements to Celsius, subtract 32 from the Fahrenheit reading, multiply the result by 5, and then divide by 9. For example, to convert 212° F to Celsius:

$$212 - 32 = 180 \times 5 = 900 \div 9 = 100°\ C$$